P9-CRT-340

The
Table Saw
Book

The Table Saw Book

Completely Revised and Updated

Kelly Mehler

The Taunton Press

Text © 2003 by Kelly Mehler
Photographs © 2003 by The Taunton Press, Inc.
Illustrations © 2003 by The Taunton Press, Inc.

All rights reserved.

The Taunton Press, Inc., 63 South Main Street, PO Box 5506,
Newtown, CT 06470-5506
e-mail: tp@taunton.com

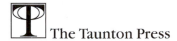The Taunton Press

Distributed by Publishers Group West

EDITOR: Paul Anthony
COVER AND INTERIOR DESIGN: Susan Fazekas
LAYOUT: Rosalie Vaccaro
ILLUSTRATOR: Mario Ferro
PHOTOGRAPHER: Terry Nelson, except where noted

Library of Congress Cataloging-in-Publication Data
Mehler, Kelly.
   The table saw book / Kelly Mehler. -- Completely rev. and Updated.
       p. cm.
Includes index.
   ISBN 1-56158-426-6
   1. Circular saws. 2. Woodwork. I. Title.
   TT186 .45 2002
   684' .083--dc21   2002009355

The following manufacturers/names appearing in *The Table Saw Book* are trademarks:
Altendorf®; Amana Tool® Corp.; Biesemeyer®; Brett-Guard®; Bridge City Tool
Works®; Bridgewood®; CMT® USA; Craftsman®; Delta®; DeWalt®; Emerson™;
Excalibur®; Felder®; Fenner Drives®; Freud® USA; General® International; Grizzly
Industrial®; Guhdo®-USA, Inc.; Hammer® USA; HTC® Products, Inc.; Incra®
Tools; Jointech®, Inc.; Makita® USA; Martin™; Oliver®; Oneida® Air Systems;
Plexiglas®; Porter-Cable®; Powermatic®; Random House®; Ridgid®; Ryobi® Power
Tools; Sawstop™; Sears®; Shopsmith®, Inc.; Starrett®; Teflon®; Tenryu® America;
Unifence®; UniGuard®; UniSaw®.

A NOTE ABOUT SAFETY:
Working with wood is inherently dangerous. Using hand or power tools improperly or
ignoring safety practices can lead to permanent injury or even death. Don't try to
perform operations you learn about here (or elsewhere) unless you're certain they are
safe for you. If something about an operation doesn't feel right, don't do it. Look for
another way. We want you to enjoy the craft, so please keep safety foremost in your
mind whenever you're in the shop.

Printed in the United States of America
10 9 8 7 6 5 4 3 2

Acknowledgments

The editors at The Taunton Press have been supportive, helpful, and more than patient with my schedule. My editor, Paul Anthony, has had the most direct impact on this book's revision. Paul's nearly daily wordsmithing, organizational skills, and woodworking insights have helped make this revision a reality. Thanks, Paul!

As you will see from this book's photography, the keen and creative eye of Terry Nelson has brought the biggest change to this edition. He has been a treat to work with and has been more than accommodating with his time.

I have been helped again by a number of tool company representatives, including Nita Miller (Biesemeyer Manufacturing); Jim Forrest Sr. & Jr. (Forrest Manufacturing); Garry Chinn (Inca-Garrett Wade); Tim Hewitt (HTC); Phil Humphrey (Exactor); Wayne Johnson (Excalibur); Wolfgang Geiger (Felder USA); Torbin and Benjamin Helshoj (Laguna); Todd Houston, Jim Parks, and Carl Merhar (DeWalt); Dave Hazelwood (Ridgid); Steve Quayle, Scott Box, and Todd Langston (Delta/Porter-Cable); Doug Colmar (Powermatic); and John Otto (Jet Tools). There are numerous other folks who have contributed in small but important ways. My thanks to them as well.

Contents

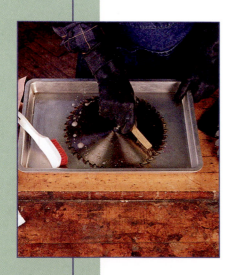

Introduction

What a great opportunity to be able to write a second edition of *The Table Saw Book*! There have been a number of changes in the world of table saws and accessories since the first edition was published in 1993.

One of the most surprising changes has been the upsurge of interest in table-saw safety. Hundreds of people have contacted me with questions, comments, and—most poignantly—their personal stories. I have been touched and moved to action by the phenomenal impact that a one-second close encounter with a table-saw blade can make on a person's life. As a result, you'll find throughout this book the best safety information currently available to help you perform your work safely, accurately, and conveniently. As you'll see, I've covered the latest in commercial blade covers and splitters. I've also provided many suggestions for crafting your own simple safeguards.

The sections on table-saw tune-up and maintenance have been thoroughly revised, organized, and expanded to give this all-important topic its due. After all, if your saw isn't properly tuned up and maintained, you're compromising the quality of your work, as well as your personal safety.

I've addressed European table saws and combination machines more often in this edition, and for good reason. These tools are making major inroads into the American market due to the space economy that they offer the small shop. As I discuss, they also typically feature superior safety equipment.

So whether you're a novice woodworker or a seasoned professional, you'll find this new edition brings you up to date on the latest developments in the world of table saws. Of course, there is also plenty of meat-and-potatoes technique to help you build your furniture, which is what you bought your saw for, after all. The complete index will help you locate the information you need, and the Sources section will help put you in touch with manufacturers of saws and accessories.

Introduction to the Table Saw

The table saw is one of the most important and versatile power tools for anyone who works with wood, from carpenters to furniture makers. It's the tool that allows you to rip, crosscut, and join wood or sheet goods most efficiently. If you are new to the craft of woodworking, a table saw will most likely be your first major power tool.

Although the table saw was originally invented to do rip cutting (that is, cut wide boards into narrower pieces along their lengths), it didn't take long to see the advantages of using this saw to make accurate crosscuts as well. For the most part, the table saw's purpose—to efficiently and accurately cut wood of almost any size—remains the same today as it did years ago.

Different types of table saws are marketed for various levels of use and expertise. There are saws for the home hobbyist, the carpenter or contractor, the small production shop, and large industry. But whatever the saw, the basic working principles are the same. A motor spins a circular saw-blade, which protrudes through a table, and the workpiece is moved through the blade.

In this chapter, I'll discuss the functions of the various table-saw parts to give you a basic understanding of how the saw works. I'll also discuss the types of saws in brief, and what they were designed for. In the next chapter, I'll delve into much more detail about the advantages and disadvantages of the particular types of saws and their features to help you in your purchasing decisions.

Basic table-saw design hasn't changed much in the days since this classic old Oliver® saw was made.

Table-Saw Anatomy

All table saws share standard features, although the design, materials, and quality vary from model to model. The basic external features include a base, a table and its extensions, rails and a rip fence, a miter gauge, a throat plate, adjustment wheels, and a power switch (see the illustration on p. 6). The internal parts include the motor, trunnion brackets, carriage assembly, arbor and arbor assembly, and sector gears (see the illustration on p. 7).

THE BASE

As its name implies, the base, or body, of the saw supports the table. It is freestanding or is used in conjunction with a stand that is positioned at an average comfortable working height of about 34 in. The base contains the internal mechanisms and incorporates the adjustment wheels and power switch. Some bases house components for efficient dust collection, but many just serve as dust containers.

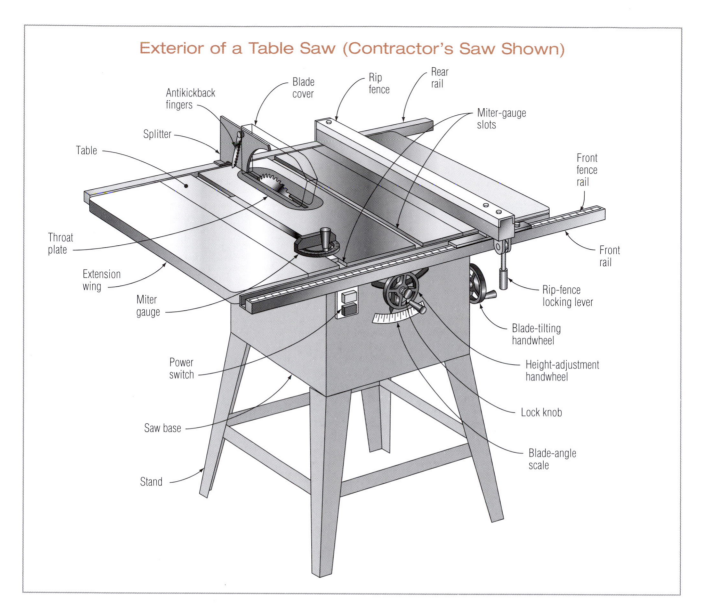

Exterior of a Table Saw (Contractor's Saw Shown)

Antikickback fingers

Blade cover

Rip fence

Rear rail

Miter-gauge slots

Splitter

Table

Front fence rail

Throat plate

Extension wing

Miter gauge

Front rail

Rip-fence locking lever

Power switch

Blade-tilting handwheel

Height-adjustment handwheel

Lock knob

Saw base

Blade-angle scale

Stand

The base protects the working parts of the machine from damage and prevents the operator from getting caught by the revolving parts of the machine. The body is generally made of steel—with thicker-gauge steel used in higher-quality saws. The bodies on some portables are made of high-impact plastic designed to withstand rough treatment and extreme weather conditions.

THE TABLE AND EXTENSIONS

Ideally, the table on a saw provides a stable, durable, flat working surface for the workpiece to ride on as it is presented to the sawblade. For the saw to cut correctly, the table surface must be as flat as possible. Therefore, heavy cast iron is the material of choice for most table-saw surfaces

Interior Mechanisms (Contractor's Saw Shown)

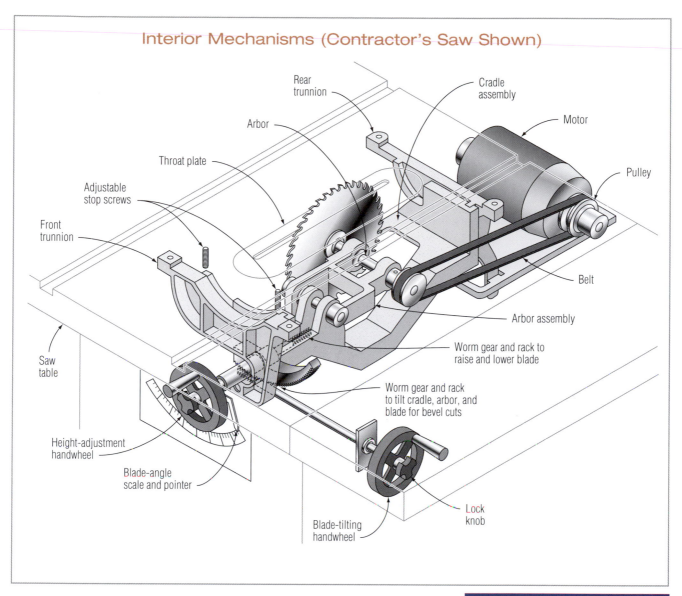

Rear trunnion

Arbor

Throat plate

Adjustable stop screws

Front trunnion

Saw table

Height-adjustment handwheel

Blade-angle scale and pointer

Blade-tilting handwheel

Cradle assembly

Motor

Pulley

Belt

Arbor assembly

Worm gear and rack to raise and lower blade

Worm gear and rack to tilt cradle, arbor, and blade for bevel cuts

Lock knob

because it provides an extremely flat and durable surface. Its weight also adds stability to the saw and helps absorb vibration. The less vibration, the longer any machine tool will maintain its accuracy. Minimal vibration also helps reduce operator fatigue.

Because a flat table surface is of paramount importance to accurate sawing, today's manufacturers of iron table-saw tops use precise technology in the production processes (see the sidebar on p. 8). The end result of careful iron manufacturing processes is a table saw that is accurate and durable enough to give generations of service.

Table extensions increase the size of a top, making large workpieces more manageable. The extensions, often called "wings," add 16 in. to 20 in. to the width of a top and increase stability by adding weight to the

Table Extensions

Shopmade table extensions can increase the effective table size of any saw, allowing you to more easily cut large stock and sheet goods.

At the Foundry

A GOOD CAST-IRON TOP can give generations of service. Today's manufacturers of cast iron can maintain precise control in the chemistry of iron composition. Better electric furnaces, modern patterns, and machining processes can provide the end user with a top that is within 0.005 in. flat over its entire surface. The level of control is such that there is no longer any reason to "cure" the iron after casting to relieve stresses. Formerly a standard practice, the curing process could add as much as a year to the manufacturing time.

When the consideration is table-saw portability, the table surface is made from cast-aluminum alloys, which are much lighter than cast iron. Anodizing the aluminum increases durability, and a coating such as Teflon® can be added to the surface to aid in hardening and to reduce workpiece friction. Even precision-machined aluminum won't make as flat or durable a tabletop as cast iron, but it provides an economical, sufficiently accurate, lightweight alternative.

Tabletops on European saws tend to be long and narrow. Instead of incorporating a fixed center top with a left hand, a long sliding table on the left of the saw carries the workpiece across the blade.

Webbed cast-iron extension wings provide a compromise between stamped-steel wings and solid cast-iron wings. They're flatter and more solid than stamped steel, but less expensive than solid cast iron.

saw. On saws other than portable saws, the table-saw surface consists of a main center section measuring about 21 in. by 27 in. The wings are bolted onto either side. On larger stationary saws, the wings are made of cast iron. On smaller home-shop saws, cast iron may be an option, but less expensive stamped-steel extensions are more common. Another option may be cast-iron wings in a "webbed" style (see the photo above). The webbed style is a compromise that provides stiffness, weight, and a flatter surface than stamped steel.

European table-saw tops differ from North American saws in that the center section tends to be smaller from side to side but deeper from front to back. The extra depth, which adds support for the workpiece, is a European safety requirement. The table extension is added to the right side of the saw. To increase the width to the left, European manufacturers typically add a sliding table that doubles as an efficient crosscutting solution (see the photo at left on the facing page).

THE THROAT PLATE

The throat opening in a tabletop is large enough to allow access for blade changing, arbor maintenance, and, on some saws, adjustment of the guard assembly. The throat plate is a separate, removable insert that sits in the throat opening, surrounding the blade. The throat plate is made of a soft, nonferrous material that won't spark or damage the blade if it comes into contact with it. A stock throat plate has a slot opening that is long enough and wide enough for the blade and a splitter or riving knife to pass through it at any angle or height.

Leveling screws in the throat plate sit on cast pods in the opening to allow height adjustment of the plate relative to the tabletop (see the photo below). The throat plate may also have one or more screws or a clip to secure it, as required on Canadian saws. Optional throat plates with wider openings are available for use with dado heads or molding heads. And custom throat plates are easy to make from plywood, plastic, or other materials.

The leveling screws in a throat plate allow for adjusting its height level to the tabletop.

European-style fences can be retracted to align with the blade for safe ripping of reactive boards that splay apart once past the blade.

The fence rails on this Inca table saw can be adjusted to the right or left to accommodate cutting on either side of the fence.

THE RIP FENCE AND RAILS

The rip fence guides wood parallel to the blade as the wood is being cut along its length, a process known as ripping. The fence head is made of metal and rides on the rails. The fence body has a facing of plastic, aluminum, or laminated wood. Some facings are adjustable to the table surface and may be replaceable. On European saws, the fence body can be pulled back to align with the beginning of the sawblade for safe ripping of warp-prone boards (see the top photo on the facing page).

The fence moves along one or two fence rails that are attached across the front and the back of the table-saw top. The length of the rails determines the ripping capacity of the saw, with 24 in. to 52 in. being the standard. A measurement scale attached to the front rail is used in tandem with a cursor on the fence head to set the fence a specific distance from the blade. Some table saws have sliding rails that can be adjusted to the left or the right to give maximum cutting capacity to either side of the sawblade (see the bottom photo on the facing page).

A clamping lever or knob on the head of the fence locks the fence to the rails. The lever or knob works by means of a cam that pushes against the front rail when the lever or knob is tightened. On some fence systems, locking the front also pulls on a rod that tightens a J-clamp on the rear rail to help secure the fence. Some fences have a microadjust knob that allows dialing in fine adjustments rather than tapping the fence into position.

THE MITER GAUGE AND MITER SLOTS

The miter gauge is used to guide the workpiece during most crosscutting operations, usually at 90 degrees. The miter gauge on most saws consists of a soft, cast-metal protractor head attached to a length of ¾-in.-wide bar stock. The head pivots on the bar to the left and right for cutting angles from 30 degrees to 90 degrees in either direction. The gauge can be locked anywhere in between these angles using the calibrated protractor scale. Most models have adjustable stops at the most frequently used angles of 45 degrees and 90 degrees.

The miter gauge slides in slots that are milled in the tabletop parallel to each other to the left and right of the blade. On most U.S. saws, the slots are fairly standard at ¼ in. wide and ⅜ in. deep. Most miter-gauge guide slots are in the shape of an inverted T to accommodate a washer that's screwed to the bottom of the miter-gauge bar at its far end. This arrangement traps the end of the bar in the slot, preventing the gauge head from dropping when pulled out in front of the saw.

Most European-style miter gauges come equipped with a long, adjustable extruded-aluminum fence facing. The facing provides added support for the workpiece as it approaches and meets the blade. European-style miter gauges are typically equipped with adjustable drop stops that ride in a T-channel in the top of the body (see the photo on p. 12). These miter gauges are supplied with European saws that don't have sliding tables. Saws with sliding tables incorporate an adjustable fence that travels with the sliding table for crosscutting operations.

Modern Rip Fences

The Achilles heel of many an early-model table saw was its troublesome, inaccurate rip fence. These days, most new saws come with premium-quality fences.

European-style miter gauges include a longer fence for better bearing and integral flip-down stops for repetitive cutting.

Trunnion Styles

The connection between the front and rear trunnion contributes to accurate cutting. A one-piece cast-trunnion assembly is preferable to trunnions connected by rails, which can flex, affecting the cut.

INTERNAL MECHANISMS

Underneath the saw table lie the parts and mechanisms that permit the machine to cut wood at varying heights and angles and allow the motor to transmit power to spin the sawblade. A good understanding of how these parts work together is essential for maintaining a safe and well-tuned table saw.

Arbor assembly The arbor assembly is at the heart of the internal mechanisms. The assembly includes the arbor and the sector gear for raising and lowering the blade. The arbor is a metal shaft that holds the blade as well as its driver pulley(s). Depending on the drive system, one or more pulleys are located either at the end of the arbor opposite the blade or at the center of the arbor. The blade end of the arbor is threaded to accept a nut that sandwiches the blade between a removable outside flange and a fixed inside flange. The pulley or pulleys attached to the arbor drive the blade by means of a motor and belt(s). Portable saws, by contrast, are direct drive, meaning that the arbor is directly attached to the motor shaft.

On most portable saws and all home-shop and 10-in. cabinet saws, the arbor is ⅝ in. in diameter. On some saws, the arbor diameter is larger through the bearings and then turned down to a smaller diameter at the blade end, allowing for a more stout arbor and bigger bearings. Table saws with 12-in.-dia. blades use a 1-in. arbor at the blade end. The most common European arbor diameter is 1³⁄₁₆ in. (30mm). The length of the blade end of the arbor can vary—an important consideration when thinking about mounting a wide dado or molding head.

Carriage assembly The carriage assembly, also referred to as the cradle, consists of the front and rear trunnions and the yolk (or rails) that connects them. The carriage assembly also serves as the mounting for the arbor assembly and motor, keeping them aligned as the carriage assembly is tilted. The carriage assembly rides in channels, or ways, milled into the trunnion brackets. The front trunnion includes a sector gear for tilting the assembly.

A one-piece, solid-cast trunnion assembly is preferable to one that uses rails to connect the trunnions because the rails can cause some twist when tilting the unit. A one-piece assembly can also more easily incorporate an efficient dust port in the casting.

Trunnion brackets The trunnion brackets at the front and rear of the saw support the carriage assembly and allow it to be tilted. On home-shop saws, the brackets are bolted to the underside of the table (see the illustration on p. 7). On stationary saws, they are secured to the cabinet itself. The trunnion brackets are most commonly made of heavy cast iron on stationary saws and lighter-weight cast iron on home-shop saws. Other lightweight metals are used on portable saws.

Sector gears A table saw has two arc-shaped sector gears for adjusting the blade. The arbor-sector gear is part of the arbor assembly and provides for raising and lowering the blade. The bevel-sector gear, part of the carriage assembly, allows tilting of the blade for beveling. Teeth on the sector gears mesh with, and are driven by, worm gears on the ends of the handwheel rods. Better saws include an adjustment on either the sector gear or the worm gear to minimize backlash between the two. Most saws include an adjustable stop at either end of the bevel-sector gear to stop the blade at exactly 45 degrees and 90 degrees.

Adjustment wheels Changes in blade height and angle are accomplished by means of handwheels that extend through the saw body. The height-adjustment handwheel is at the front of the saw body. It is used to raise and lower the blade and can be prevented from turning by using the locking knob at its hub.

The blade-tilting handwheel is located either on the right or left side of the saw base on most home-shop and stationary saws. On portable saws, it is located on the front of the saw where it is combined with the height-adjustment wheel. The blade-tilting handwheel is used to tilt the blade for bevel cuts and to set the blade at 90 degrees to the tabletop for square cuts. The handwheel has a corresponding degree gauge, typically on the front of the saw base, that indicates the approximate cut angle. Like the height-adjustment handwheel, the blade-tilting handwheel has a locking knob at its hub. For some high-end saws, an optional dial indicator is available for clear indication of the exact blade height and angle.

Power switch The power switch is located on the front of the saw. Switches come in various sizes, shapes, and colors, but there are two basic mechanisms: magnetic and manual. The contacts on a magnetic switch are maintained by electric current only, whereas a manual switch maintains an electrical contact by physical pressure.

The important difference lies in the way that the switches react to a power failure. If the power fails (due to a tripped circuit breaker, for example), a magnet switch will automatically disconnect and remain off until the "on" button is pressed again. This ensures that the saw doesn't jump back to life on its own when the power returns—a potentially dangerous risk that you run with a manual switch. A magnetic switch is required on any table saw in a commercial or educational setting. Switches that can be shut off with the press of a knee are required on table saws in Europe.

Basic Safety Equipment

The table saw is a tool with great potential—for both creativity and accidents. Manufacturers recognize the dangers and provide basic safety equipment on every table saw they sell. The stock safety equipment on saws sold in the United States is somewhat similar to that on European saws, but it differs in name and ease of operation. Standard safety equipment includes a blade cover, a splitter or riving knife, antikickback fingers, and belt and pulley guards. (For a more detailed discussion of safety features, see chapter 4.)

Accessible Controls

Large handwheels and an easily accessible power switch contribute to safe, convenient saw operation.

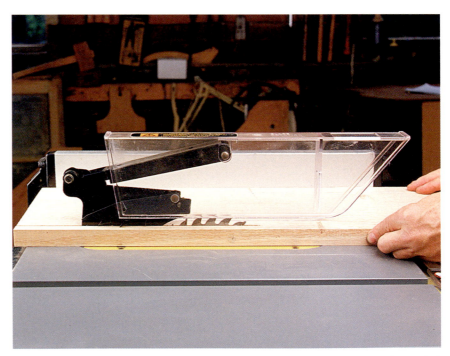

The blade guard on a typical American saw is made of metal or clear plastic and is attached to the flat metal splitter that projects up through the saw's throat plate.

BLADE COVER

The blade cover, sometimes called a blade guard, helps to prevent your hands and other objects from accidentally meeting the blade. The blade cover also deflects away from the operator the wood chips and sawdust thrown by the blade. The cover may be made from clear plastic, metal, or a combination of metal and plastic (see the photo on the facing page). A good blade cover surrounds the blade but does not interfere with normal cutting operations.

SPLITTER OR RIVING KNIFE

A splitter or riving knife is a piece of metal located directly behind and in line with the blade. It is crucial to the safe operation of a table saw. It denies the workpiece access to the rear saw teeth, which can cause it to be picked up and thrown violently toward the operator—a dangerous situation known as kickback. It also helps prevent reactive wood from pinching the blade, causing it to bog down or burn the wood. (Read more on kickback and safety in chapter 4.)

ANTIKICKBACK FINGERS

Antikickback fingers, or pawls, are a safety addition on saws sold in the United States. Antikickback fingers are normally attached to the splitter but are sometimes part of the guard. The sharp fingers allow the workpiece forward motion by pivoting out of the way, but supposedly prevent reverse motion by digging into the workpiece if it is forced backward. European safety standards don't require antikickback fingers.

BELT AND PULLEY GUARD

On a contractor's saw, which has an exposed motor, a belt and pulley guard keeps objects (and fingers) from getting caught up between the belt and the pulley during operation.

Types of Table Saws

With the burgeoning interest in woodworking as an American pastime, the types, features, and even names of table saws are changing at a fast pace. It is exciting to see saws developed and introduced into the market with features that are better able to meet the needs of all the various people who work with wood. In addition to the usual selection of saws available on the U.S. market for years, we're beginning to see the introduction of more European saws, giving us the chance to learn how European woodworkers approach safety and versatility issues.

   The descriptions that follow provide an overview of the types of saws currently available to help you understand their purposes and basic features. In the next chapter, I'll discuss their features in much more detail and address changing terminology in the field of table saws.

Blade Guards

Stock blade guards are often poorly designed, as explained in chapter 4. Before buying a particular saw, consider the future costs of upgrading it with good aftermarket safety accessories.

The portable saw is a light- to medium-duty tool, popular with do-it-yourselfers and job-site carpenters.

PORTABLE SAWS

Portable table saws are small, lightweight machines that are designed to be carried by one person (see the photo at left). Portable saws come without legs and are meant to be clamped or bolted to a commercial or shopmade stand or work surface. Even though portable saws are diminutive in size, they are capable of most of the operations of larger saws.

The portable saw is a direct-drive tool. Instead of a separate arbor assembly and arbor that is driven by a motor, the shaft on the motor is the arbor. Unlike the heavy industrial direct-drive machines of old that used a large induction motor, the portable table saw uses a small, lightweight universal motor. Universal motors are used in portable hand tools of modest power, such as routers, circular saws, and drills. The largest of these motors on a table saw can handle a 10-in. blade and can cut softer woods at full height, but they have trouble doing so on hardwoods.

The smallest portable saw is the model maker's saw. As its name implies, it is a craft-specific tool. Sizes for these saws run from 2 in. to 4 in. (With table saws, size refers to blade diameter.) The most powerful model maker's saws will cut 1-in.-thick balsa or basswood and ¼-in.-thick hardwood, depending on the type of blade used. The model maker's saw can be belt driven or direct drive. It is not unusual for the saw to have variable speeds spinning from 3,500 rpm to 7,000 rpm for cutting nonferrous metals, wood, and plastics.

The next largest portable saw is a lightweight saw with minimal extras. Often called a benchtop saw, it has the basic features of any table saw—a fence, a miter gauge, and a tilting arbor—but all have been reduced in size and weight. This saw has an 8-in. or 10-in. blade and a small motor. The benchtop saw is suitable for the do-it-yourself home handyperson with limited space, a tight budget, and perhaps minimal needs for a table saw. As small as this tool is, it can still be a handy tool for light-duty work.

The largest portable saw is designed with the carpenter or contractor in mind. This user needs a saw that is truly portable but that can cut the size and type of materials used in the building trade. Manufacturers have supplied this market with 10-in. portable saws that offer extended capacity fences, larger and flatter work surfaces with expandability, and strong motors. Even with all of this, manufacturers have kept the weight to under 70 lb.

HOME-SHOP SAWS

The type of saw used most often by serious home woodworkers was originally designed for the contractor during the housing boom that took place right after World War II. This table saw was a scaled-down version of the very large industrial table saw. At the time, this "contractor's saw" seemed light in comparison with the industrial version. Even though it weighed in at more than 200 lb., it could be moved as necessary by a couple of stout

The traditional contractor's saw is still popular today with many home-shop woodworkers.

Price vs. Value

In general, the cost of a more expensive saw buys you increased accuracy, power, and durability.

workers. The motor that hangs out the back is removable to make transportation easier.

Today, contractors use portable saws unless the job demands finer finish work. What is commonly known as a contractor's saw is actually a full-sized saw with a medium-weight, cast-iron table (see the photo above). The cabinet is attached to an open stand constructed of sheet steel. This saw uses standard 10-in. blades and will accept a host of accessories. Contractor's saws are adequately powered for cutting dimensional lumber, but the typical 1½-hp motor often labors when cutting heavier hardwoods. The motor is mounted on a pivoting frame at the back of the saw cabinet and delivers power to the saw arbor by a single belt.

Some manufacturers are recognizing the need for a saw specifically designed for the home woodworker and have created a saw for the home shop. This saw tucks the motor back into the cabinet, thereby freeing up shop space and giving the saw better balance and reduced vibration. Home-shop saws come with features such as accurate fence systems, improved dust collection, and sturdier bases.

CABINET SAWS

Cabinet saws are considered stationary saws. The primary difference between these saws and home-shop saws is their weight. Intended for heavy-duty use, a cabinet saw doesn't normally get moved around in the shop. In its standard configuration, the footprint of a cabinet saw is really no bigger than the previous saws mentioned. But in weight these saws can be 200 lb. to 600 lb. heavier.

The cabinet saw is the choice of professional woodworkers due to its accuracy, stability, and power.

The extra weight on a cabinet saw is due to its beefier parts. The thicker cast-iron top and extension wings, heavier cast internal mechanisms, larger motor, thicker enclosed base, larger adjustment wheels, fence, and even the miter gauge all contribute to the extra weight (see the photo above). The components on the cabinet saw are heftier and machined to closer tolerances, resulting in a saw that is more accurate and stable. The larger internal mechanisms are built to handle a more powerful motor and to run longer with less vibration.

Cabinet saws are powered with motors in the 3-hp to 5-hp range. The motor used is a totally enclosed, fan-cooled (TEFC) unit, which makes for a longer life inside a dusty saw cabinet. The motor drives the arbor using two or three short belts to eliminate belt slippage and deliver maximum power. Short belts also create less vibration and noise than the long belts on home-shop saws. As their name implies, cabinet saws have a fully enclosed cabinet, to which the saw table is attached. The cabinet also adds heft and stability to the saw, and because it encloses the motor and internal parts, it muffles some of the noise and contains the sawdust.

EUROPEAN SAWS

European table saws differ from their American counterparts in two distinctive ways. The first is that their safety and dust-collection features are much more effective. The second is that these saws incorporate a sliding table, which makes handling of large workpieces such as sheet goods much easier.

The sliding-table design came about as a direct result of the devastation of Europe in World War II. The scarcity of trees and need for rebuilding after the war demanded more efficient use of wood in the form of plywood and other sheet goods. That, in turn, prompted the development of saws that could more easily handle sheet goods.

A sliding table is basically a platform that easily carries a workpiece past the blade—a much better alternative to pushing a workpiece with a miter gauge. On most European saws, the sliding table is an integral part of the machine. On a few saws, the table is an add-on, often called a rolling table. An integral table is preferable because it comes right up to the blade, providing a more accurate and safer way to cut any workpiece. An add-on sliding table is adequate for many operations but not as precise. Sliding tables are available in various sizes. Larger tables are capable of carrying sheets up to 5 ft. wide and 10 ft. long.

COMBINATION MACHINES

Combination machines incorporate a number of woodworking machines in one package. These machines typically include the five most commonly used stationary tools in woodworking: the table saw, jointer, planer, shaper, and horizontal mortiser. All five tools can be combined in a machine that takes up less space than two table saws placed side-by-side (see the photo below).

These machines are masterpieces of economy. Each individual tool shares space, capacity, mass, and features with other tools on the machine. The best combination machines come from Europe, where space is a luxury in short supply and the demand for quality is high. Sizes and capacities of combination machines vary to meet the needs of the small home shop or large professional shop.

A combination machine offers a table saw, jointer, planer, shaper, and horizontal mortiser all in one relatively compact, high-quality package.

2

Buying a Table Saw

A table saw is an investment, so it's important to make a wise choice when buying one. Your decision will depend largely on your budget, the type of work you want to do, your available workspace, and how often you'll be using the saw. In this chapter, I'll try to help you work through those variables. I'll discuss ways to match your needs and resources to the right table saw for you.

My first suggestion is that you read chapter 1, if you haven't already. It presents a good overview of table-saw types and features that I'll be discussing in more depth in this chapter. A familiarity with the basic capacities, features, strengths, and limitations of the various types of saws will provide you with a base of knowledge for your decisions.

What Size Saw?

The size of a saw technically refers to the largest blade it will handle and thus its cutting depth—an important consideration. However, the size of the machine itself and the power of the motor are just as important as the blade size. It's these three factors together that basically define the various types of saws, as I'll discuss here.

PORTABLE TABLE SAWS

The last few years have seen the introduction of a lot of new portable saws. Although they're often called benchtop saws, you wouldn't use one on a typical benchtop (see the sidebar on the facing page). These saws are great for cramped shops and garages and can easily be stowed away when not in

Not a Benchtop Saw

PORTABLE SAWS, SOMETIMES CALLED benchtop saws, aren't really made to use on top of a typical bench, which would put them too high for comfortable, safe operation. For many models, an accessory stand is available, but you could make your own stand instead. Although you could size the stand to create the standard saw-table height of 34 in., you may want to customize the stand to suit your particular height instead. Ideally, the tabletop should be at the same height as your palms when extending your fingers out parallel to the floor.

Portables Need Tuning

When you buy a portable table saw, be prepared to spend time addressing flaws and shortcomings right out of the box, as a fair amount of fine-tuning may be required to make it perform well.

A portable saw can be quickly set up anywhere, making it ideal for job-site work.

use. They're also turning up more and more on job sites, gradually replacing the traditional contractor's saw.

Portable-saw design has greatly improved over the last few years. Recent models have flatter tops, more power, larger blade capacity, more accurate fences, and improved dust collection. On higher-end portable saws, the mechanical systems are being manufactured to closer tolerances, minimizing vibration and making for easier operation overall.

A good tool for carpentry and basic cabinetmaking, the portable saw is suitable for cutting building-supply lumber and lightweight sheet goods. In general, it's well suited to handling stock less than 1 in. thick and shorter than 4 ft. long. Ripping thick hardwood is possible, but it will tax the motor. By setting up outfeed supports, sheet goods can be cut easily and fairly accurately.

As good as the portable saw has become, it's still not suited for the kind of precise cutting demanded by furniture making. This is not to say

SAWBLADE CUTTING CAPACITIES

The size of a blade determines the thickness of stock it can cut.

Blade Size	Cutting Capacity at 90 Degrees	Cutting Capacity at 45 Degrees
8 in.	2¼ in.	1⅝ in.
10 in.	3 in.	2¼ in.
12 in.	4 in.	3 in.

The blade on a portable saw is mounted on an arbor that's directly connected to the motor shaft.

Of Table Saws and Toasters

WHEN IT COMES TO QUALITY, I'm the kind of guy who will wait and save up for a well-made, well-designed tool rather than just buying whatever I can afford immediately. You might laugh if I tell you that I spent more than $100 for a toaster some time ago. But it's made well, does its job faithfully, and will long outlast the seven before it that ended up in the trash.

As a furniture maker, I'm willing to invest in a table saw with features that will make for easier, more accurate, and safer work. I can justify the cost of a strong, precision machine that will handle anything I feed it and will hold its settings over time. Even though you may not have the cash or space for a full-sized top-of-the-line table saw, you should buy the best you can afford within its class. As with most purchases, the added initial cost of higher quality usually means greater savings and satisfaction down the road.

Unfortunately, many of us tend to focus on price rather than on quality features and construction. I think that's one of the reasons for the shortcomings on so many saws sold in the United States: We're not willing to invest in safety, accuracy, efficiency, and quality, so few tool dealers here offer that standard of equipment. In the United States, we think $2,000 buys a real top-of-the-line table saw, when in fact we're often getting shoddy safety "features" and a saw that isn't easily capable of crosscutting large stock or panels.

It's odd that many woodworkers who balk at spending a few thousand dollars for a lifetime table saw think nothing of ponying up nearly that much every few years for a new computer system that will have almost no resale value in a few years. To add to the irony, if we add up the money we end up spending on accessories such as a better fence, blades, guards, belts, dust collection, and a sliding table, we probably could have bought the saw that was properly designed with all those features to begin with.

Of course not everyone needs a top-of-the-line saw. But if you consider yourself a serious woodworker and intend to be at it for some years, well, do the math.

that it takes a big, heavy, expensive saw to do fine work. I've seen some beautiful, precise work come off of small, inexpensive tools. Tuning up the saw and working within its capabilities can give you good results. However, you may have to spend more time setting up for each cut than you would with a stationary saw.

The overall lightweight construction of portable saws contributes to vibration, causing saw parts to wear and jiggle out of alignment over time. And these saws—all of which are driven by a universal motor—are definitely underpowered when it comes to cutting thick stock, especially hardwoods. They're not intended for hogging a lot of wood. In fact, most won't even accept full-width dado heads.

Portable saws are direct drive. That is, the blade is mounted to an arbor that's connected directly to the motor shaft (see the photo on the facing page). Although horsepower ratings often aren't stated, motors typically range from 12 amps to 15 amps (see the sidebar on p. 35). These motors are very loud and demand ear protection, probably for your neighbors as well.

Portable saws are relatively inexpensive, ranging from about $300 to $500. The more expensive models have more capacity and include better features.

HOME-SHOP TABLE SAWS

The next step up from a portable saw is a home-shop saw, sometimes referred to as a contractor's saw (see the sidebar on p. 32). These saws are engineered more solidly than portable saws for more serious use and increased accuracy.

Weighing from 200 lb. to 300 lb., a home-shop saw can be moved by two people to a job site if necessary. On traditional contractor's saws, the motor hangs out the back for easy removal for transportation. On some new home-shop saws, the motor is enclosed in a cabinet. As on portable saws, the motor trunnion assembly on home-shop models is attached to the tabletop, although the cast parts are built heavier.

A home-shop saw is well suited to cutting sheet goods as well as most dimensional lumber, although it's underpowered for sawing thick hardwood.

Replacing the Rip Fence

If you already have an older contractor's saw with a stock fence that isn't straight and easily adjustable, consider installing a good aftermarket fence, which will greatly improve the accuracy of your work. You could also add an aftermarket sliding table to extend the saw's crosscutting capabilities.

Compared with portable saws, the tables on home-shop saws are larger and flatter and the fences are longer and sturdier, so they'll handle large stock better, especially sheet goods (see the photo on p. 23). Of course, you'll still need to use outfeed support of some kind.

The saws generally come outfitted for a 24-in. ripping capacity, but you can order a longer fence and rail system as part of a package that offers extended side support and ripping capacities. Alternatively, you could upgrade later with an aftermarket fence system.

Home-shop saws are good for every type of woodworking from carpentry and cabinetmaking to furniture making. They provide a good compromise between a portable saw and a cabinet saw. They are the least expensive saws you can use for serious woodworking. A home-shop saw is stronger and more accurate than a portable saw, but not as strong or accurate as a cabinet saw. Part of the compromised accuracy has to do with the design of the carriage assembly to the tabletop (see the illustration on p. 7). The mounting can cause the blade to shift slightly out of alignment to the miter-gauge slots when it's cranked over for miter or bevel cuts.

Home-shop saws are powered with induction motors, which are quieter, stronger, more efficient, and more durable than universal motors. A belt connects a pulley on the motor to a pulley on the arbor shaft to drive the blade (see the photo on the facing page). The arbor shaft is long enough to accept dado and molding heads.

A home-shop saw typically comes equipped with a dual-voltage 115/230 volt, 1½-hp motor that is prewired for 115 volts. This allows you to plug it into any standard 15-amp household outlet. However, if your saw is dedicated to your shop use, it's wise to rewire the motor for 230-volt usage, which will maximize the motor's efficiency and minimize possible voltage drops. Of course, you may then need to wire your shop for a 230-volt electrical outlet if you don't already have one. It's not wise to replace the 1½-hp motor with a much larger one, because the internal mechanisms on the saw weren't designed to handle it.

At 1½ hp, the motor is a bit underpowered for cutting thicker hardwoods. However, it should serve fine for most lumber and all sheet goods. If you're taxing the motor, try a slower feed speed, a thin-kerf blade, or multiple shallow passes. If you overheat the motor, its internal circuit breaker will trip, and the motor must cool before you can reset it.

The extended motor on a traditional contractor's saw hinders dust collection because of the open base that allows the motor to project. The fact that it hangs out the back also makes the saw tippy, especially when cutting heavy sheet goods. And the long belt contributes to vibration. The traditional contractor's saw was really designed for the job site, not the shop, and I'm glad to see some new thinking in the design of saws for the home woodworker.

Home-shop saws are powered with an induction motor that drives the blade via a belt. Motors on some newer home-shop saws hang inside the cabinet instead of out the back of the saw.

Home-shop saws range in price from $500 to $1,000. Many package deals are available that include your choice of several different fences, as well as extension tables, a mobile base, a sliding table, and cast-iron extensions to replace the stock stamped-steel wings.

A cabinet saw is a strong and accurate machine, well suited to professional woodworking.

CABINET SAWS

If you're a serious professional woodworker or simply aspire to professional-quality work, you'll want a cabinet saw for its strength and accuracy. A good cabinet saw will work all day long cutting anything you put to it, including thick hardwoods and sheet goods (see the photo above). Tuned up properly, it will handle all sorts of precision joinery while holding its mechanical settings. Named for its enclosed base, a cabinet saw is designed to stand up to the rigors of years of work in factories and commercial shops. It's substantial and heavy and is often called a stationary table saw.

Cabinet saws are available in several sizes, with 10 in. and 12 in. being the most common. Because of their weight and heavy construction, cabinet saws have a very stable footprint and negligible vibration in use. They tend to have flatter tables and extensions than portable or home-shop saws. Table sizes vary, but they're about the same as table sizes on home-shop saws.

These days, cabinet saws come equipped with top-of-the-line fences and long fence rails for wide ripping capacity. Some manufacturers offer optional sliding-table accessories as an add-on, although none compare with an integral sliding table like those on European saws that come right up to the blade. Any cabinet saw can be retrofitted with an aftermarket sliding table, but that's going to jack up the overall cost of your saw to nearly that of a lower-end European saw. So if a sliding table is important to you, you might consider getting a European saw to begin with (see "European Saws" on p. 28).

A 3-hp to 5-hp induction motor enclosed in the base drives the arbor shaft via a wide belt or multiple belts for great power transmission. And because the motor is enclosed in a base, a cabinet saw runs quieter than saws with open bases. The enclosed base also keeps a majority of dust from spewing out into the shop, although in itself, that's not a very elegant solution for dust collection. An optional port is usually available for connection to a dust collector, but even that isn't generally very efficient.

The heavy-duty trunnion-and-motor assembly attaches to the base rather than to the tabletop as in home-shop and portable saws. This makes alignment of the miter-gauge slots to the blade much easier and ensures that the blade will stay parallel to the miter slots even when it's cranked over for bevel cuts. To drive these large motors, you'll need a 230-volt circuit, which isn't a big deal for an electrician to install if you need one.

Three-phase power is also an option. Three-phase motors run more efficiently, last longer, and are cheaper. Unfortunately, three-phase power isn't typically available in most residential neighborhoods, but you can convert an existing 230-volt circuit to three-phase by installing a converter.

You can buy a decent cabinet saw in the United States for somewhere between $1,000 and $2,000, but expect to pay at least $2,000 for the better models. Although relatively expensive, a cabinet saw is a reasonable business investment and tends to maintain a good resale value over time. Investigate the accessories you might want and see if you can get a good package deal by buying them at the same time that you get the saw.

Magnetic Switches

All cabinet saws come with magnetic safety switches that prevent a motor restart after a power interruption—a great safety feature should the power go out mid-cut and you forget to turn off the saw.

EUROPEAN SAWS

European saws are distinctively different from their American counterparts in several ways, primarily in their well-executed safety features and their ability to handle and crosscut large workpieces due to the sliding table incorporated into most of these saws (see the photo on the facing page). Another important difference is that the typical European table saw is designed to accommodate a number of accessory machines such as a jointer/planer, shaper, and a horizontal mortiser. A European table saw has plenty of power for cutting even thick hardwoods due to its large, 230-volt motor.

The woodworking trades in Europe have great influence regarding the safety standards required for woodworking machines. As a result, the safety features on European saws are well designed and effective. For example, the riving knife doesn't impede the feeding of a workpiece, as does the splitter on so many saws sold in the United States. And a safety brake that stops a spinning blade seconds after switching off the saw also helps prevent accidents.

Most European saws include an integral sliding table as stock equipment. With a few models, the table is available only as an add-on, which is sometimes called a rolling table due to its significantly different mechanisms for movement. Integral tables work better because they are incorporated into the design of the saw and include a much more sophisticated guiding system. The table itself extends all the way to the blade, which means that the workpiece is carried entirely by the sliding table. The add-on sliding tables don't provide as much accuracy due to their particular mechanisms and attachment to the saw.

Regardless of the type, a sliding table provides enormous advantages for the furniture maker. Pushing a workpiece across the saw table with a miter gauge is no comparison with carrying it effortlessly through the blade on a sliding table. Accuracy, safety, and capacity are all greatly improved. Sliding tables are available in various lengths, typically ranging from 3 ft. to 10 ft. (front to back). A 4-ft.-long table suits most general woodworking just fine. However, longer tables open more possibilities for ripping, as well as handling full-sized sheet goods.

Some American woodworkers may lament the inability to mount a dado or shaper head on a European saw. The arbor isn't long enough to accommodate these tools because their operation is considered unsafe in Europe. Grooves and dadoes there are typically cut on the shaper.

The typical European table saw (including the sliding table) can cost from $2,000 to $5,000 in the United States. These saws are initially more expensive than their American counterparts, but if you factor in the cost of all of the aftermarket accessories necessary to bring a U.S. table saw in line with a Euro saw, the cost may not be all that different. And with a European saw the accessories are all designed as integral to the machine, making it that much better than an aftermarket-accessorized saw.

The sliding table on a European saw makes handling of large workpieces easy. The sliding table rides right up next to the blade. An outrigger (the green extension shown here) carries the bulk of the workpiece.

European-Style D.I.Y.

THE MARKET IN EUROPE for home-woodworker equipment is much smaller than in the United States. Even so, many tools are available for the do-it-yourself (D.I.Y.) homeowner, as well as the contractor who needs a portable job-site saw.

The smallest European portable table saws actually consist of a portable circular saw that's inverted and attached to a stand that incorporates a rip fence and miter gauge. You'll also find some of the same portable saws in Europe that are sold in the United States, since many have been made to CE (European safety) standards—unlike most of the cabinet and contractor's saws sold in the States that don't even come close to meeting CE standards.

PANEL SAWS

A panel saw is a basically a large sliding table saw designed to handle primarily full-sized sheet goods. The sliding table is always integral—never an add-on. A full-sized outrigger table for panel support is carried by a telescoping arm. The sliding table has a stroke of at least 8 ft., and a 10-ft. stroke isn't unusual. A panel saw always includes a scoring blade that is powered by a separate motor. The main blade is 10 in. or 12 in. in diameter. Many European saws and combination machines are available in panel-saw configuration. Manufacturers such as Altendorf® and Martin™ are well known for their premium panel saws. The cheapest panel saw available is about $6,000.

Combination Machines

I had always thought of combination woodworking machines as cheaply made tools that probably didn't perform any of their functions particularly well. But after being introduced to European combination machines, I've changed my thinking radically. In fact, most of these machines are elegantly designed to incorporate various top-of-the-line woodworking tools in one space-saving package (see the photo below). More and more woodworkers in the United States—including serious nonprofessionals—are buying combination machines for use in small shops, garages, and basements.

The typical combination machine combines a sliding table saw, a shaper, a jointer/planer, and sometimes a horizontal mortiser. Changing from one function to another generally takes less than a minute. Because the setup of one tool can affect another, you learn to plan the sequence of

A fully outfitted combination machine combines a table saw, a shaper, and a jointer/planer all in one space-saving package.

MEETING YOUR MATCH IN A TABLE SAW

Type of Saw	Capabilities	Pros and Cons	Comments
Portable saw	Do-it-yourself home projects; carpentry and trim work; basic cabinetry.	**Pros:** Portable; inexpensive. **Cons:** Very loud; vibration-prone; hard to keep well tuned; under-powered for cutting thick wood.	Good choice for the job site or a cramped shop. Don't expect great accuracy from these saws.
Home-shop saw	Carpentry and trim work; cabinetry; basic furniture making.	**Pros:** Semiportable; decent power and accuracy; accepts a premium fence **Cons:** Underpowered for cutting thick hardwood; open-base models hinder dust collection.	The basic table saw for the home woodworker. A good compromise between a portable saw and a cabinet saw.
Cabinet saw	All types of woodworking including professional furniture making.	**Pros:** Powerful, accurate, and stable; comes with a premium fence; the cabinet helps retain dust. **Cons:** Expensive; difficult to move.	The North American benchmark in a commercial/ industrial saw.
European saw	All types of woodworking including professional furniture making.	**Pros:** Powerful, accurate, and stable; sliding table enables accurate, convenient crosscutting of long stock and sheet goods; good safety features. **Cons:** Expensive; difficult to move; no dado capacity; weak rip fence.	May well represent the model for the next advances in U.S. table-saw design.
Combination machine	All types of woodworking including professional furniture making.	**Pros:** A great shop-space saver; add-on machines are typically of the same high quality as the core table saw. **Cons:** Expensive initial cash outlay; use of some tools involves a changeover.	Basically a European table saw with other machines added to it.

your processes more than you might with stand-alone tools. Occasionally, a change-over will cause the loss of a previous setting, such as that of the rip fence, but I haven't found that to be a regular problem when working with my combination machine. You can't use more than one function at a time on these machines, but that is seldom an issue in a one- or two-man shop.

The jointer/planer unit utilizes the same cutterhead, which is typically at least 12 in. long. To change over from jointing to planing capability, you simply lift the jointer tables and flip up a dust-collection hood. The jointer/planer on many models can be separated for use as a stand-alone

Unlike many table saws sold in the United States, European saws and combination machines employ effective, easy-to-use guards and very efficient dust collection.

What's in a Name?

THE NAMES THAT WE'VE ALL BEEN USING TO DESCRIBE the different types of table saws are fast becoming outdated. Changes in the marketplace have resulted in major modifications to saw design, especially regarding saws targeted to the do-it-yourselfer, the serious amateur, and the contractor.

Portable Saws

The term benchtop saw has really become a misnomer as manufacturers beef up these saws, adding size, improved features, and cutting capacity while still keeping them compact and lightweight. Many now come with 10-in.-dia. blades, and I wouldn't be surprised if the 8-in. models are entirely phased out over time. Currently the more proper term is portable saw, since portability is their real benefit and the reason why they've become the sweetheart saws of the construction trades.

Home-Shop Saws

The contractor's saw was designed more than 60 years ago for the job site—at a time when carpenters spent a lot more time building a home than they do today. Sort of a stripped-down model of a cabinet saw, it was the lightest saw available, even at more than 200 lb. By extending the motor—one of the heaviest components—out the back, it could be removed easily for transporting. When aspiring home-shop woodworkers went looking for a table saw, this was the most suitably priced, although it was never designed to be a home-shop saw.

Many traditional-style contractor's saws are still available, but improved designs are starting to surface. These updated versions often include a motor that's housed in a stand or cabinet, a more refined fence system, and better safety and dust-collection features. All of these saws, including the contractor's models, are more appropriately called home-shop saws.

Cabinet Saws

Cabinet saws are also known as stationary saws. A long time ago, they were called circular saws as they still are in Europe. However, that term in the United States has come to designate hand-held circular saws. The term cabinet saw came about as a way to distinguish these saws from contractor's models. Cabinet-saw design hasn't changed a lot over the years except that the base, which used to be made from cast iron, is now made from sheet steel.

machine if you choose to place it elsewhere. (On moving day, you'll be relieved to know that most combination machines can be broken down to fit through a typical doorway.)

The weight of the total machine is collectively shared for each function, adding to the overall stability of each tool. The shaper, for example, effectively enjoys the weight and large footprint of a table saw, eliminating the vibration you might expect from a stand-alone shaper. The shaper also makes use of the sliding table.

ALTHOUGH THE VAST MAJORITY OF TABLE saws come with a right-tilting blade, some are available with a left-tilting blade. Whether a left- or right-tilt blade will serve you better depends on the type of work that you primarily do. As a solid-wood traditional furniture maker for more than 23 years, I have found that a right-tilting blade has worked just fine for me. However, a friend of mine who does a lot of architectural woodwork swears he couldn't operate without a left-tilting saw.

The issue mostly has to do with cutting bevels. When ripping bevels, it's not a safe practice to trap the workpiece between the fence and the "underside" of the angled blade (see the illustration at right). In this situation, the blade wants to shoot the workpiece back toward the operator. Also, when ripping or crosscutting bevels, a workpiece under the sawblade will tend to burn if any inconsistencies in the thickness or flatness of the material cause it to push upward against the spinning blade.

Instead, for a safer and cleaner cut, you want the bevel of the workpiece on the "upper" side of the tilted blade. With a right-tilt saw, this means moving the fence to the left side of the blade. This is fine for workpieces less than about 12 in., which is the typical maximum ripping capacity to the left of the blade. Your stance when ripping on the right side of the fence may feel a bit awkward, but the operation is safe as long as you use a blade guard and splitter or riving knife.

The main advantage of a left-tilting blade is the ability to cleanly and safely bevel-rip wide panels because you can rip on the left side of the fence as usual. The main disadvantage is that a left-tilting table saw does not work well with a sliding table, which would trap the workpiece under the angled blade. (If you use a miter gauge instead of a sliding table, you'll run the gauge in the right-hand miter-gauge slot of a left-tilting table saw.)

My advice would be that if you have a choice between a left-tilt and a right-tilt saw and all other features are equal, get the left-tilt saw as long as you're certain that you are not going to add a sliding table eventually.

Ripping Bevels

Incorrect: The workpiece is trapped under the tilted blade.

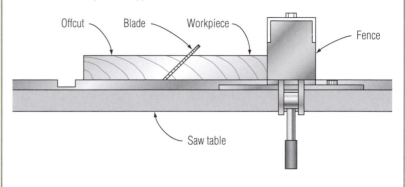

Offcut   Blade   Workpiece   Fence   Saw table

Correct: The workpiece is against the fence and not trapped under the blade.

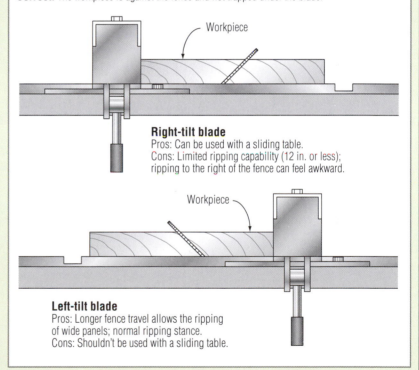

Workpiece

Right-tilt blade
Pros: Can be used with a sliding table.
Cons: Limited ripping capability (12 in. or less); ripping to the right of the fence can feel awkward.

Workpiece

Left-tilt blade
Pros: Longer fence travel allows the ripping of wide panels; normal ripping stance.
Cons: Shouldn't be used with a sliding table.

A full-function combination machine typically has three separate motors: one for the table saw, one for the shaper, and one for the jointer/planer. (The optional horizontal mortiser mounts on the end of the jointer/planer cutterhead.) You have a choice of motors, ranging from 3 hp to 10 hp. A start/stop switch is mounted at each function. As a safety feature, any of the stop switches will shut off all machine functions. The motors are wired to run on 230-volt current, which is standard household current in Europe. Three-phase motors are also an option, as are inverters that allow you to run 3-phase motors on 230-volt current.

For increased space efficiency, optional mobility kits are available for attachment to a combination machine. The kits typically consist of two heavy-duty casters that attach to one end of the machine and a single caster on the opposite end that can be raised and lowered with a lever so you can move the beast when needed. At least one model offers a turnstile option, which allows you to rotate the machine in place when necessary. This can be helpful, for example, when the machine is near a wall and you need more infeed and outfeed area in a certain direction.

Full-function combination machines (with a sliding table saw, a shaper, and a jointer/planer) can range anywhere from about $5,000 for the economy models to as much as $30,000 for a full-featured, top-of-the-line model with maximum capacities.

Features to Consider

Once you've decided what type of saw will suit your work and pocketbook, it's wise to compare features within that class. Decide which features are most important to you, then get the best quality you can in that area. For example, if you work with heavy material, you may be more concerned with power and having a large, sturdy table. Or you may be more concerned with dust collection because you care about your health and shop environment. Whatever your focus, here are some guidelines to help you choose the best saw for you.

POWER AND CUTTING CAPACITY

In general, the more powerful a saw, the fewer its limitations. Once you've decided on the class of saw you want, compare motor specifications between models. But don't be misled by horsepower ratings; compare amperage ratings instead (see the sidebar on the facing page). All else being equal, get the saw with the most power. A 3-hp motor will provide enough power to cut just about all woods using a 10-in. blade. You'll need a 5-hp motor to power a 12-in. blade for the same purposes.

The cutting capacity of a saw is determined by the diameter of the blade as well as the length of the fence rails and any sliding table or extension tables. If you work with a lot of thick stock, you'll want a 10- or

Motor-Power Ratings

IN GENERAL, THE MOTOR THAT COMES WITH A SAW is designed to suit the mechanisms and capacities of that saw. For example, a 10-in. saw is designed and built to handle a blade no larger than 10 in. in diameter. It takes more power and bulkier machine parts to power a larger blade that is meant to cut thicker material. I've found that a 1½-hp motor is the smallest acceptable motor on small saws. It takes a 3-hp motor on a 10-in. saw to provide the power it needs to cut through thick hardwoods. For a 12-in. saw, you'll need a 3- or 5-hp motor.

Motor power can vary from saw to saw within a given class of saw. When investigating motors, don't be misled by "peak" ratings, which indicate maximum horsepower under no load. "Rated" horsepower is more relevant because it indicates horsepower under load.

In any case, horsepower isn't the best gauge of motor power, and it's often not listed in a saw's specifications anyway. The better gauge for motor power is the amperage rating, which you should find on the motor plate if it's not listed in the saw's specs. The more amperage a motor draws, the more power it has. For general reference, 13 amps is equal to about 1 hp on a universal motor and about 1½ hp on an induction motor.

12-in.-dia. blade as well as a strong motor (see the chart on p. 22). If you use a lot of sheet goods, you'll need a sliding table and/or a fence that will adjust at least 50 in. from the blade to allow you to saw to the center of a full sheet of plywood.

FENCE AND RAILS

A premium-quality rip fence can make your work a lot more accurate, efficient, safe, and enjoyable. Not long ago, these fences were only available as replacement, aftermarket accessories. But woodworkers and tool manufacturers alike have come to realize the importance of a good-quality fence that is straight, flat, and easily adjustable. These days, most table saws come with premium fences (see the photo on p. 36). For those that don't, and for older saws, many models are available as aftermarket accessories.

Setting up an old-style stock rip fence can be a real chore. It usually requires measuring and remeasuring at both ends of the fence for each new cut to make sure the fence is parallel to the blade. This fussiness led to the development of many precise aftermarket fence systems, including the Accufence, Biesemeyer®, Excalibur®, Paralok, Unifence®, and Vega, among others sold on the U.S. market (see Sources on p. 197).

European safety standards require that fences on European saws have the capability to be set in both a high and a low position. (The Delta® Unifence available in the United States is a good example of Euro-style fence design. However, the Unifence is solidly constructed, as opposed to some stock fences on European saws, which may flex somewhat.)

The premium fences that come with most table saws today are solid, straight, and easily adjustable. They stay parallel to the blade and can be set by using an integral cursor and scale, rather than by measuring for each cut with a tape rule from fence to blade.

When set in its low position, a European-style fence allows more room to maneuver your hand and push stick for ripping narrow stock (see the photo on the facing page). The low position is also used for ripping bevels with the fence to the right of the blade (see "Ripping Bevels" on p. 142). The fence can be set to act as a half-fence, locking it in place with the far end of the fence aligned to the front teeth of the blade to prevent kick-back when ripping reactive wood (see "A Half-Fence" on p. 126).

It's important that a fence stay parallel to the sawblade at any position on the fence rails, and a premium fence ensures that. One of the other biggest advantages is the time saved setting up a cut. Instead of measuring from the blade to the fence, you simply line up a cursor on the body of the fence with the measurement scale on the fence rail. Rails come in various lengths; if you have the shop space, it's a good idea to get rails that will allow at least 4 ft. of ripping capacity to the right of the blade. That will make cutting sheet goods and other large work more manageable. Many fences include various other features such as microadjust mechanisms and fore-and-aft adjustment (see the sidebar on the facing page).

Premium fences range in price from about $200 to $400. Many are heavily discounted when purchased as part of a new saw package. These fence systems fit all of the popular saws except portable saws. Some fence systems require drilling holes in the edge of the saw table because the

Comparing Premium Rip Fences

A STRAIGHT, EASILY ADJUSTABLE FENCE that locks parallel to the sawblade is a table saw's best accessory and a real time saver. It makes for quick, accurate setups and easy repeatability of cuts. The popularity of these premium fences is underscored by the fact that 25 or so different models and sizes are available, either as part of a new saw package or as aftermarket accessories. Many models are available in either a home-shop or a commercial version. They are generally both of the same quality; the home-shop version is just smaller. Here are a few things to look for when choosing the right fence for your needs.

- Straightness of the fence is critical, and you'll find that most models are very straight. Some include polyethylene faces that are screwed to the main fence body to reduce friction. If you're considering one of these fences, make sure that the poly doesn't deflect around the screws, which is sometimes a problem.
- Parallelism to the sawblade is also of utmost importance for safety and accurate ripping. As long as the front rail is installed correctly, this is generally not a problem, but check that the fence stays parallel to the blade regardless of where on the rail it's locked down.
- High-low mounting allows the positioning of the fence to more safely rip thin or tall stock as needed (see the photo at right). Only Delta's Unifence and fences on European saws offer this as a built-in capability. However, you can easily outfit any fence for ripping thin or tall stock by adapting it with shopmade attachments (see "Basic Ripping Techniques" on p. 127).
- Cursors and scales need to be precise and easily readable for quick and repeatable fence adjustments. Better fences have very fine, hairline cursors and scale markings. It's best if the cursor rides close to the scale to avoid problems with parallax.
- Fore-and-aft adjustment is a feature that allows you to slide the fence to the front of the saw to provide more advance bearing surface for long stock. Aligning the rear end of the fence with the sawblade also helps when cutting reactive wood, which can warp as it leaves the blade (see "Basic Ripping Techniques" on p. 127).
- Microadjust mechanisms on some fences allow you to make very fine adjustments with the turn of a knob. I like this feature, although many woodworkers find it easy enough just to tap the fence lightly for the proper adjustment.
- T-tracks milled into the fence body allow use of proprietary and shopmade accessories such as featherboards and other hold-downs.

The Delta Unifence, as well as most European-style fences, can be mounted in low position for ripping narrow stock. This provides room to better maneuver your hands and push stick.

fence rail bolts don't always match up with the table's existing holes. All of the fence systems are fairly easy to install in a few hours at most.

TABLE SIZE AND MATERIAL

The size of a saw table determines how comfortably and safely the saw will handle larger stock, particularly sheet goods. In the shop, you can easily enlarge the table surface by surrounding any saw with extension tables. However, if you do a lot of job-site work, the stock table size may be more of a concern, unless you don't mind dragging along your extension tables.

Tables on portable saws are made of aluminum to minimize weight. The depth (front to back) of tables on portable saws varies from about 16 in. to 20 in. The width can range from about 26 in. to 40 in., so check the specifications on any model you're interested in. Remember, though, that a larger table may decrease portability by adding both bulk and weight to the saw. You'll have to decide whether ripping capacity or portability are more important. Even the largest table doesn't provide sufficient support for handling full-sized sheet goods without auxiliary supports.

The depth (front to back) of most home-shop and cabinet saws sold in the United States is 27 in., although there are exceptions. The width of the typical table is about 36 in. to 40 in. including its two stock metal extensions, sometimes called wings. For saws that come with long fence rails for extended ripping capacity, you can buy or make a long wooden extension table to replace the right-hand wing. Almost without exception, the main, central table on a home-shop or cabinet saw is made of cast iron. The wings can be made of solid or webbed cast iron or stamped steel.

Ideally, a table should be dead flat, but that's rarely the case, even with top-of-the-line cabinet saws. Sometimes a twisted table, or one that droops at one end, can be the result of the saw's stance on an uneven floor, and can be easily corrected. You wouldn't think cast iron would bend, but it does (see "Aligning the Tables" on p. 96).

Of more concern is a table that is dipped or humped because that's not easily remedied and can affect your cuts, depending on where the deviation is and how severe it is. For example, a dip or hump to the left of the sawblade can result in out-of-square crosscuts, but a dip at the far end of the table or somewhere else may not be an issue. It all depends on how the stock rides on the table in relation to the blade. Of course, the real test is to cut some stock, then check it with a square or ruler—whatever's appropriate.

MITER GAUGE AND MITER SLOTS

Ideally, you want a miter gauge with positive stops and a face that's square to the saw table (see the photo at left on the facing page). The bar should fit snugly in its slot but slide freely. The miter-gauge slots are actually more important than the gauge, which can be easily replaced. The slots should be consistent in width and depth and be parallel to each other.

Aftermarket Accessories

As you're deciding what saw to buy, consider what aftermarket accessories you might want down the line. If you can afford it, buy them when you get the saw. A package deal is cheaper than buying the accessories later. Don't forget to compare the total cost of the accessories you want against the cost of simply buying a better saw that includes the features as stock equipment.

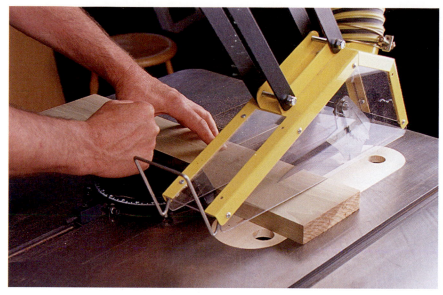

A miter gauge should lock positively at any angle. Some better-quality miter gauges have long fences and flip-down stops for accurate repetitive cuts.

I have to admit that I don't use a miter gauge at all when I need to make accurate cuts. I find that crosscut sleds work much better, providing more bearing surface for the workpiece, as well as a place to attach stops for repeatable cuts (see "Crosscut Sleds" on p. 146).

WEIGHT

One of my earliest woodworking teachers told me that you can base the value of a woodworking machine on its weight: the heavier the tool, the better. The extra mass on a machine makes it less prone to vibration, which causes parts to wear and jiggle out of alignment. Although that's generally true, if a smaller, lightweight machine is well balanced and manufactured to close tolerances, it can produce some very precise work.

CONTROLS

The location and smooth operation of a saw's switch and handwheels are important because they're used so often. A switch needs to be immediately accessible and should be very easily turned off. I particularly like knee-operable switches like the one on the left side of the DeWalt® #746 home-shop saw (see the photo at right). A switch with a mechanical lockout can be important if kids frequent your shop. Handwheels should turn smoothly without struggle. Better handwheels are large and made of metal instead of plastic.

SAFETY EQUIPMENT

The typical blade-safety device on saws sold in the United States is sort of a three-in-one device. It incorporates a blade guard (properly called a

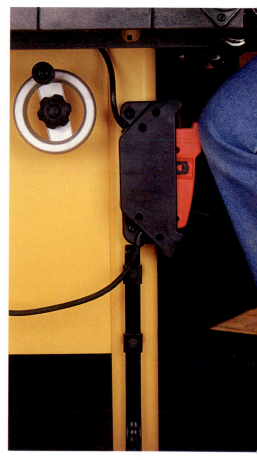

The DeWalt #746 home-shop saw can be quickly shut off using your knee—a nice safety feature.

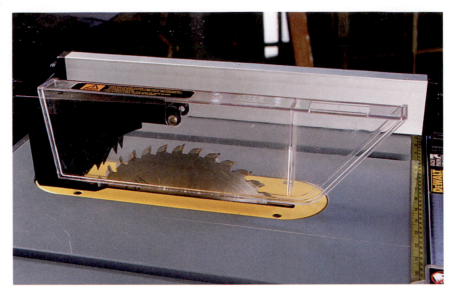

Blade safety on most U.S.-marketed saws consists of a blade cover, splitter, and antikick-back fingers all combined in one poorly designed unit.

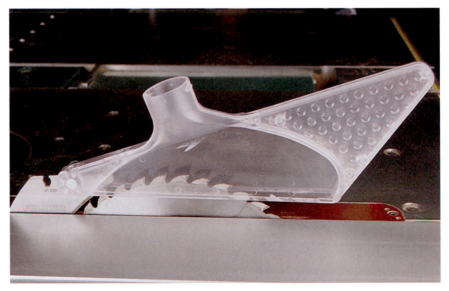

The typical European blade cover removes easily for blade changes and includes a dust port. The riving knife maintains its relationship to the blade regardless of blade angle or height.

blade cover), a splitter, and antikickback fingers all in one unit (see the top photo). Although blade-safety devices are crucial to the safe operation of a table saw, this particular configuration is poorly designed for many typical woodworking operations. It often impedes feeding of stock and is difficult to remove and reinstall when necessary for certain operations. As a result, many woodworkers remove these safety features from the saw—not a wise idea, as many scarred woodworkers will testify.

The blade-safety devices on European saws are much friendlier and better designed. For one thing, the blade cover attaches to a riving knife, rather than to a splitter, and the cover detaches easily when necessary. European saws don't have antikickback fingers but don't need them because of the properly designed riving knife. The European riving knife is attached to the arbor assembly and, once adjusted, remains in proper relationship to the blade regardless of the blade height or angle (see "Splitters and Riving Knives" on p. 67.) The blade cover also has a dust port to capture dust thrown upward (see the bottom photo on the facing page).

You can't retrofit European blade-safety devices to a typical U.S. saw, but there are other options available, such as the blade cover/splitter systems sold under various names such as Brett, Biesemeyer, Delta, Excalibur, and Exactor (see "Better Blade Covers" on p. 70). On these systems, the splitter and cover are separate, allowing more flexibility in guarding difficult cuts. Some offer dust-collection options at the blade.

DUST COLLECTION

Unfortunately, nearly all saws made for the U.S. market make little or no provision for efficient dust collection. The typical saw simply throws the sawdust into the space below the table and all over the operating mechanisms of the saw. Contractor's saws are the worst offenders, with their open backs and bottoms. You can fit optional dust ports to some of these saws, but they're not very efficient, even if you close off the open back and bottom of a saw as best you can.

Even a cabinet saw with an enclosed base isn't much more than a dust container. You can get an optional dust-collection port for many cabinet saws, but that's not a very effective solution. The dust port is really just a hole near the bottom of the cabinet. Even a good dust collector can't keep the cabinet and interior mechanisms clean; the best it can do is suck up most of the swirling dust.

The best solution for dust collection is to surround the blade below the table with a ported shroud that connects to a dust collector via a hose. This concentrates the sawdust in a small area for easy evacuation. It also takes advantage of the blade rotation, which propels the dust toward the collection hose (see the photo at right).

On smaller saws, nothing more than a shop vac is needed. Because of European safety standards, all European saws incorporate a design like this. Most of the newer portable saws and a couple of the new home-shop saws sold in the United States are featuring this design now too. Unfortunately, it would be difficult to retrofit to existing saws. (For more on dust collection, see chapter 4.)

Dust collection on European saws, such as the Inca saw shown here, incorporates a ported blade shroud that connects to a dust collector via a hose.

Getting the Scoop on Saws

THERE ARE A LOT OF WAYS to find information and specifications on new saws.

- Read tool reviews in recent issues of various woodworking magazines.
- Join a local woodworkers group and discuss various saws with those who have used them.
- Attend a local woodworking show where you can get your hands on a saw and maybe get a deal on a "show special."
- Call dealers for a catalog (see Sources on p. 197).
- Visit the manufacturers' web sites for information about their tools.
- Participate in an online woodworkers discussion group. Many have message boards dedicated to tool talk.

Specification Checklist for Buying a Saw

WHEN INVESTIGATING AND COMPARING SAWS, specifications can be found in catalogs and on manufacturer's web sites. In the case of private sellers, much preliminary information can be gotten over the phone to determine whether a saw is worth a visit. Keeping track of all this information, though, can be an organizational nightmare. Make photocopies of this checklist to help you keep the important things sorted out.

Make, model, and type: _____

New: ____ Used: ____

Dealer/seller name and phone number:

_____

Price and options included: _____

_____

Blade diameter: _____ in.   Right tilt _____   Left tilt _____

Type of fence: _____

Ripping capacity: _____ in.

Motor: _____ hp _____ amps

Table size: length _____ width _____

Enclosed base: yes _____ no _____

Dust-collection port: yes _____ no _____

Cost if optional $_____

Notes: _____

Buying a Used Saw

If buying a new saw is beyond your budget, a used saw may be the answer, enabling you to get much more for your money. For example, you should be able to buy a professional-quality used saw for the price of a brand-new home-shop saw. The difficult part can be finding a source for used machinery, but they are out there.

- Newspaper ads are a good place to start. Check the "Tools and Equipment for Sale" section in the classified ads. You might also consider placing a want ad yourself.
- Equipment auctions, also found in the classified ads, can be a good way to find table saws, particularly if a cabinet shop has gone out of business. But don't necessarily expect great deals at an auction. Tools have often been used very hard, and they frequently still go for a premium. All the same, good deals can be had for the more experienced eye.
- Used equipment dealers can be a good source of table saws if you live near a metropolitan area. Check the local yellow pages. Used saws may also be available through new-machinery outlets that take used saws as trade-ins. Although you might not get as good a deal from a dealer as from a private party, it's likely that the saw has been reconditioned and may include some kind of warranty.
- Local woodworking guilds and clubs can be invaluable resources for shared information about tools and equipment of all sorts. Members often have tools for sale or if not, know someone who does. You'll also get lots of well-founded opinions on the various saws members have used.

EVALUATING A USED SAW

When you inspect a used table saw, there are a few critical things to consider. First, always check for worn bearings or a bent arbor shaft, which are the most likely problem areas (see "Arbor and Bearings" on p. 87). Although you can replace bad bearings or a bent arbor shaft, it's a fair amount of trouble and cost. I would probably turn down any saw with these problems.

Check the flatness of the tabletop with a good straightedge (see "Aligning the Tables" on p. 96). If a top is bad enough to need regrinding to flatten it, I would look for another saw. Also inspect for cracks in the top, base, and internal mechanisms. I would probably steer away from a saw with these problems.

Try the fence and handwheels to make sure they're not jammed up. Always try to arrange for a hands-on test ahead of time, and make sure suitable power will be available. Bring along tools and wood for your test-drive (see the sidebar at right below). Many problems such as stiff gears and burned or out-of-square cuts are usually minor problems that can be solved by a thorough tune-up later (see chapter 5).

Used-Saw Inspection Checklist

WHEN BUYING A USED SAW, particularly from a private party, make sure to inspect it carefully before pulling out your wallet. There's usually a "no returns" policy. Before buying a saw with missing or damaged parts, research the cost and availability of replacement parts. Here is a list of items to check when inspecting a saw.

Make, model, and type: _____
Seller's name and phone number: _____
Price: _____
General condition of saw: (any rust pitting, dents, etc. to indicate poor care? _____
_____
Arbor and bearings: Does the arbor shaft turn smoothly without rough spots? _____
Is there any up and down play in the shaft? _____
Any worn spots or damage on the arbor? _____
Any missing parts? _____
Any cracks in the top, base, or internal mechanisms? _____
Is the top reasonably flat? _____
Does the motor sound like it's running smoothly? _____
Does it bog down under load? _____
Is the fence straight and does it lock securely to the rail? _____
Do the handwheels and switch operate properly? _____
Any damage to the teeth on the internal sector gears? _____
Is the manual available? _____
Notes: _____
_____

Test Gear

WHEN BUYING USED EQUIPMENT, it's important to check it out thoroughly because there is often a "no returns" policy. When going to test a used saw, consider bringing along the following tools and supplies to help you with your tests.

- Square
- Straightedge
- Dial indicator
- Feeler gauge
- Wrenches
- Wood with straight edges (for test cuts)
- Push sticks
- Safety glasses
- Hearing protection

Table-Saw Blades

A table saw's blade is just as important as the machine itself. To get the most from a table saw, it needs to be outfitted with a good-quality blade that's appropriate to the work being performed. But picking the right blade for the job can be confusing because there are so many different types with different tooth configurations to choose from.

In this chapter, I'll tell you how to select the right blade to suit your work and how to identify a good-quality blade. I'll also discuss specialty blades such as dado heads, scoring blades, and molding heads. Protecting your investment in blades is also important, so I'll cover blade care and maintenance as well.

Blade Design and Anatomy

A sawblade consists of three basic elements: the body, the arbor hole, and the teeth (see the illustration on the facing page). Here are some important things to look for when you are trying to decide which blade to buy.

BLADE BODY

The body of a sawblade is a steel plate that must be flat and stay stiff when in use. It is typically made of carbon-steel alloy. The flatter the plate, the smoother the blade will cut and the quieter it will run. Cheap blades are merely polished or quickly ground; better blades will show fine circular grind marks emanating from the arbor hole outward to the rim of the blade. Better blades also typically have slots cut in the body to allow the rim to expand without distorting out of flat as heat builds up at the cutting edge.

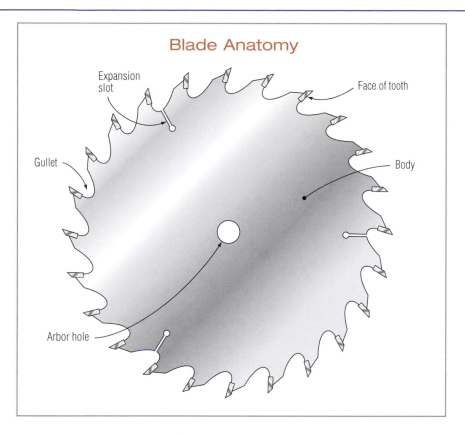

Blade Anatomy

Expansion slot

Face of tooth

Gullet

Body

Arbor hole

A good straightedge will detect serious warp in a blade.

Some sawblades for European saws include holes to accommodate brake pins on the saw arbor.

Blade warp isn't necessarily obvious; however, a bad warp can be detected by checking it with a good straightedge (see the photo on p. 45). To do this, back up the straightedge with a strong light and try to detect light between it and the plate. Test various areas of the plate. That's just a rough check, though; the best way to check a blade's flatness, or runout, is to mount it on the saw and check it with a dial indicator (see "Aligning the Miter-Gauge Slots to the Blade" on p. 100).

Any runout detected with the blade mounted on the saw will represent the combination of arbor-flange runout and the blade runout. But it's that total measurement that you're most interested in anyway, because it determines the quality of the cut you'll get with that particular blade on the saw. Runout of somewhere between 0.005 in. and 0.010 in. is to be expected. If it exceeds that, try to determine if the runout is being affected by something other than blade warp: Make sure the arbor-flange runout doesn't exceed 0.001 or that worn arbor bearings aren't causing the problem. Also check for debris between the arbor flange and the blade. If blade warp appears to be the primary problem after all, it can often be fixed by a saw smith.

ARBOR HOLE

The arbor hole should fit as snugly as possible around the arbor. A snug fit is one indication that the blade was carefully manufactured, because it's

Thin-Kerf Blades

NOT ALL BLADES ARE MADE TO THE SAME THICKNESS. Thin-kerf blades are made with thinner bodies and narrower teeth that typically cut a ³⁄₃₂-in. kerf, although the teeth on some blades are even narrower. The advantage of these blades is that they require less power to run because they remove less wood. Therefore, they're well suited to low-powered portable saws and contractor's saws. The disadvantage of a thin-kerf blade is that the thin plate is more prone to vibration, causing it to run less true and cut less cleanly than its thicker counterpart. It can also be noisier and more prone to heating up quickly.

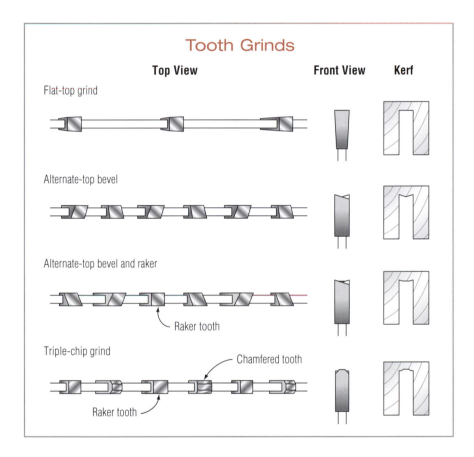

Tooth Grinds

	Top View	Front View	Kerf

Flat-top grind

Alternate-top bevel

Alternate-top bevel and raker
— Raker tooth

Triple-chip grind — Chamfered tooth
— Raker tooth

easier and quicker to make an oversized hole than one that's precisely sized. On some inferior blades, you can see a metal lip or burr where the hole was simply punched through. On better blades, the hole is first laser-cut undersized, then reamed out to within 0.001 in. to 0.0015 in. oversize, leaving a smooth, clean-edged hole. Some European sawblades include holes that slip over short posts on the arbor flange called brake pins (see the photo on the facing page).

Buy Good Sawblades

With sawblades, you generally get what you pay for. As a reference, the 10-in., 40-tooth, ATB blades most highly recommended by seasoned woodworkers cost around $100.

Carbide vs. Steel

NOT VERY LONG AGO, STEEL BLADES were the only choice for the table-saw owner. However, with the development of tungsten carbide, steel blades have been almost totally replaced in the modern woodshop by blades with carbide teeth. Tungsten carbide is an extremely hard alloy formed by bonding tungsten, carbon, and cobalt.

Although carbide blades are more expensive than steel blades, the higher initial cost is more than offset by the carbide's longevity, low maintenance, and cutting performance. A carbide blade can cut smoothly up to 50 times longer between sharpenings when cutting hardwoods, and up to 400 times longer when cutting man-made materials such as particleboard. Today, when choosing a blade for your table saw, it's not really a choice between steel or carbide; it's a matter of what to look for in a carbide blade.

TEETH

Sawblades employ variations on four teeth configurations, called grinds (see the illustration on p. 47). The four configurations are called flat-top grind (FTG), alternate-top bevel (ATB), alternate-top bevel and raker (ATB&R), and triple-chip grind (TC). The teeth on a typical carbide-tipped sawblade are ⅛ in. wide, producing a ⅛-in.-wide cut, or kerf. Each type of tooth configuration has its own particular strengths and applications. I'll focus on carbide-tipped blades here because steel blades are of little real use to woodworkers these days (see the sidebar above).

Flat-top grind (FTG) Flat-top grind teeth have a flat face and a flat top. FTG teeth are primarily rip teeth and work like a chisel, cutting well with the grain but poorly across the grain. A blade designed for ripping generally has 24 to 30 FTG teeth, with deep gullets between the teeth to eject the large chips produced and to cool the blade body. Because of the grind of the teeth, an FTG blade doesn't produce a very smooth cut, but it's the best blade to use for fast, heavy-duty ripping.

Alternate-top bevel (ATB) The teeth on an alternate-top bevel blade are ground at alternating angles. ATB teeth slice through the wood with a shearing action, producing a cut with little or no tearout across the grain. On some blades, the angle of the bevel may be as little as 5 degrees, but on others, it may be as much as 40 degrees. Teeth with steeper bevels produce less tearout, but they dull more quickly.

General-purpose combination blades—which work well for both ripping and crosscutting—employ the ATB grind. Although these blades do not rip as quickly as an FTG blade with fewer teeth, they will rip a smoother cut without too much more feed force. They also won't cut as smoothly as a crosscut blade with a greater number of ATB teeth, but they do cut with a minimum of tearout in both solid wood and sheet goods.

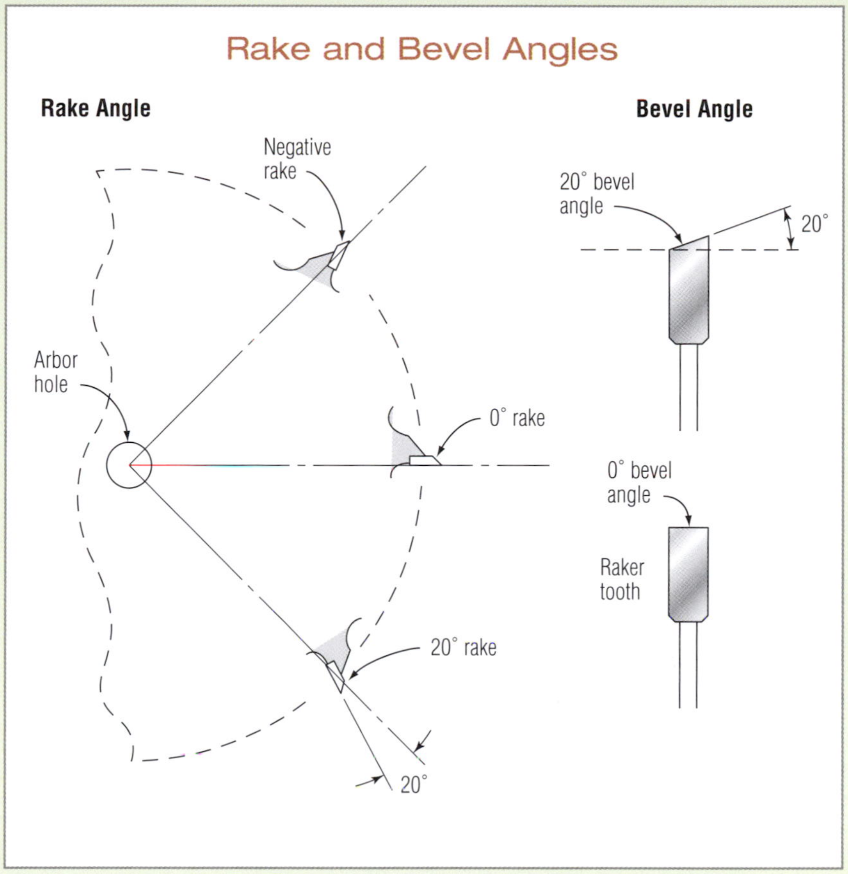

THERE ARE TWO ANGLES TO A TOOTH THAT DETERMINE ITS FUNCTION. The first, called rake, is the angle at which the body of the tooth attacks the workpiece. The second, called the bevel angle, is the angle across the top edge of the tooth.

The rake, or hook, angle is determined by drawing a line from the center of the blade to the tip of a tooth (see the illustration at right). A tooth whose face is parallel to that line has a 0-degree rake. If the face of the tooth leans forward of the line, it has a positive rake. If it leans backward, it's considered a negative rake.

The greater the rake angle, the more aggressive the cut, but also the more tearout you'll get on the exit side when crosscutting. A blade with a lower rake angle will give you less tearout when crosscutting, but will require more feed pressure when ripping. For ripping, a 15-degree to 20-degree angle is about right. For crosscutting on the table saw, 10 degrees to 15 degrees is fine. Blades with a 0-degree or negative-degree rake are designed for radial-arm saws and sliding compound miter saws to prevent the blade from driving the saw carriage forward too aggressively.

The bevel angle is the angle ground across the top of the tooth. A tooth with a 0-degree angle is straight across and is represented by the teeth on an FTG blade. This is the most efficient design for ripping, as the entire edge of the tooth splits the wood along the grain as it enters the workpiece. But this also produces a rough cut and tearout when crosscutting. The bevel angle of teeth on an ATB blade typically ranges from 10 degrees to 20 degrees. The steeper the angle, the cleaner the cut because the point of the tooth scores the wood fibers just before the bevel shears the wood. The tradeoff is that a steeply angled tooth dulls more quickly.

Rake and Bevel Angles

Rake Angle

Negative rake

Arbor hole

0° rake

20° rake

20°

Bevel Angle

20° bevel angle

20°

0° bevel angle

Raker tooth

Teeth: More or Less

BECAUSE 10-IN. BLADES ARE THE MOST COMMON, all of this talk about the number of teeth on a blade refers to 10-in. blades. To do the same job, an 8-in. FTG blade might have the same number of teeth, but a 12-in. FTG blade might have six more. For ATB blades, figure about 10 fewer teeth for an 8-in. blade and about 10 more for a 12-in. blade. These figures are all relative, of course. There seem to be very few standards when it comes to sawblades.

A 40-tooth ATB blade is the one that you'll want on your saw most of the time.

Alternate-top bevel and raker (ATB&R) As its name implies, an alternate-top bevel and raker blade incorporates both alternate-top bevel teeth and raker teeth. A typical 10-in. blade consists of 10 groups of five teeth separated by deep gullets. Each group is made up of four ATB teeth preceded by a raker tooth. ATB&R blades are the original "combination" blades, created for both ripping and crosscutting. However, the design is basically a carryover from old steel-blade technology and is fast being superseded by the 40-tooth ATB blade.

Triple-chip (TC) On a triple-chip-grind blade, the corners of every other tooth are chamfered at 45 degrees. The teeth in between are either flat-top rakers or ATB teeth. Each chamfered tooth plows a rough center cut, which is then cleaned up by the rakers. Trip-chip blades are designed for cutting dense man-made materials such as particleboard, plastics, and aluminum because the raker-style teeth won't dull as quickly as beveled ATB teeth. TC-grind blades will do an acceptable job on solid wood but typically won't cut as cleanly as an ATB blade.

Selecting the Right Blade for the Job

The proper blade for the job depends on the type of material to be cut. When working with solid wood, it also depends on the kind of cut you want to make (see the chart below). Here are some guidelines.

SOLID WOOD

For ripping operations, I typically use two types of blades. At the beginning of a project, when sawing a lot of boards to rough sizes, I use a 24-tooth FTG blade (see the photo on p. 52). This blade requires less feed force than a blade with more teeth and is sturdy enough to saw through thick hardwoods. It also saves my smoother cutting blade. The

MATCH THE BLADE TO THE JOB

Type of Cut	Appropriate Blades
Solid-wood ripping	FTG (24 to 30 teeth) ATB (40 teeth)
Solid-wood crosscutting	ATB (40 to 80 teeth)
Plywood	ATB (40 to 80 teeth)
Particleboard, MDF, plastic laminate	TC (80 teeth)
Melamine	TC (80 teeth) ATB (40 to 80 teeth)
Plastics, nonferrous metals	TC (80 teeth)

Use a piece of scrap wood or a wooden throat plate to stabilize the blade as you remove the arbor nut.

Commercially made plastic covers are available to protect your blade and hands when changing the blade.

TO CHANGE THE BLADE ON A TABLE SAW, disconnect the power to the saw, then remove the throat plate. Use a wrench to loosen the arbor nut. (I replace the stock, stamped-steel blade wrench with a better-fitting wrench with a longer handle.) If the arbor has left-hand threads, as most right-tilt saws do, the nut is removed by turning it clockwise. A left-tilt saw arbor has right-hand threads, so the nut is removed by turning it counterclockwise. Regardless of the tilt of the blade, you'll always pull the wrench toward the front of the saw to loosen the nut.

I wedge a piece of scrap wood or my wooden table-saw insert against the teeth of the blade to hold it while I turn the nut (see the photo at left above). Alternatively, you could use a rag or a commercially made plastic cover (see the photo at right above). To prevent the nut from falling into the sawdust at the bottom of the saw, place your finger on the end of the arbor and unscrew the nut onto your finger.

Next, remove the washer and the blade, being careful not to cut yourself. Be sure to set the blade

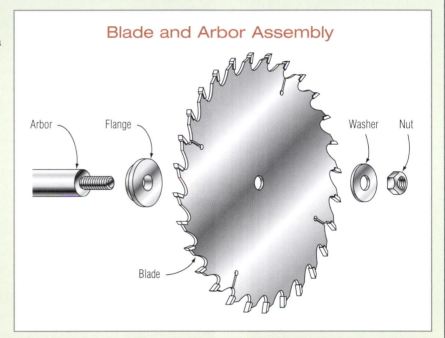

Blade and Arbor Assembly

Arbor   Flange   Washer   Nut

Blade

down on a piece of wood to prevent the teeth from chipping on the metal saw table. Install the new blade on the arbor, making sure that the blade's teeth face toward the front of the saw. Replace the washer and the nut, then tighten the nut snugly but not too tightly. Again use a piece of scrap wood to hold the blade stationary. Finally, replace the throat plate.

Testing for Tearout

To really test a blade for tearout, try cutting a piece of oak plywood across the grain. If the exit side of the cut is clean, you've got a good cross-cut blade.

A 24-tooth FTG blade (foreground) serves for fast ripping. A 40-tooth ATB blade (center) does a good job of both ripping and crosscutting. The 80-tooth ATB blade (rear) crosscuts with little or no tearout.

24-tooth blade does leave some saw marks, but that's not an issue at this point because the boards have to be ripped to final size later anyway, at which point I'll use a 40-tooth ATB blade.

For most crosscutting, I use a premium-quality 40-tooth ATB blade, which is the blade that lives on my saw most of the time. When I need an especially clean cut with no tearout, I switch to an 80-tooth ATB blade.

PLYWOOD

Many kinds of hardwood plywood—particularly close-pored woods like birch and maple—can often be cleanly sawn using a sharp 40-tooth ATB blade. However, for cutting oak plywood and other panels with tearout-prone face veneers, use an 80-tooth ATB blade for a clean cut.

OTHER SHEET GOODS

Particleboard, medium-density fiberboard (MDF), melamine, and plastic laminates are all dense materials that can quickly dull sawblades. Although you can cut these panels with a 40-tooth ATB blade, it's best to use an 80-tooth triple-chip blade, which stands up better to the wear.

PLASTICS AND NONFERROUS METALS

Woodworkers occasionally find themselves needing to cut acrylic, other plastics, and nonferrous metals such as brass and aluminum. Although the table saw isn't necessarily the best tool for cutting plastic and metal, it will do the job. Use an 80-tooth triple-chip blade because of the tough, dense nature of these materials.

Gauging Blade Quality

The quality of sawblades varies greatly. In general, you get what you pay for. For the sake of comparison, I'll separate blades into three broad categories: premium blades, mid-grade blades, and economy blades.

PREMIUM BLADES

Premium blades are made to close tolerances and high standards so that they can endure the fast, continuous pace of a heavy production shop. The manufacturing time and labor are reflected in the prices, which typically range from $75 to $200. One indication of a well-made blade is the quality of the brazing that connects the tooth to the plate. The brazing will be smooth without pits or gaps, and the tooth will be smooth and finely ground (see the photo below). The arbor hole will fit the saw arbor snugly without slop and the blade body will often include expansion slots to dissipate heat. The teeth will be sharp and polished, and the blade will be very flat.

One indication of a premium blade is smooth, nonpitted brazing where the tooth attaches to the plate of the blade.

A Basic Blade Set

SO HOW MANY BLADES DO YOU REALLY NEED? That depends, of course, on the type of work you do. If you do general woodworking, cutting primarily solid wood but also some plywood and particleboard, a good-quality 40-tooth ATB blade would be your best first choice. A good second blade to have would be a high-bevel 80-tooth ATB blade for making fine crosscuts and sawing plywood. After that, you could fill out your set with a 24-tooth FTG blade for fast, easy ripping, particularly of hardwoods.

If you work with a lot of dense, man-made boards like particleboard, MDF, plastic laminates, and solid-surface material, your choices would be different. Your blade set might consist of a 40-tooth ATB blade for general wood cutting, followed by a 60- to 80-tooth TC blade for the man-made boards. You might then add a high-bevel 80-tooth ATB blade for sawing tearout-prone panels like melamine and oak plywood.

By the way, don't throw out the typically inferior blade that came with your saw. It can be very handy for cutting through the occasional dirty, nail-ridden board.

MID-GRADE BLADES

Although not quite as durable as premium blades, mid-grade blades are a good value if you aren't involved in heavy production woodworking. These blades are probably the best choice for the serious home woodworker or small-shop professional. You can often get a good deal on mid-grade blades from mail-order suppliers, with prices in the $40 to $75 range; some higher-end blades sell for $80 to $100.

ECONOMY-GRADE BLADES

Economy blades are manufactured to minimum standards for those who want to buy as cheaply as possible, regardless of quality. The blades may have pitted teeth and a rougher finish than mid-grade blades, and they aren't machined as carefully. To me, economy blades are just a waste of money. They cost $40 or less, and after a couple of sharpenings should be thrown away.

Specialty Blades

In addition to the standard blades described above, there are a number of specialty blades designed for specific operations. These include stacking and adjustable dado blades for cutting dadoes and grooves, and molding cutters for shaping the edges of boards into decorative profiles.

DADO BLADES

Dado blades—also called dado heads—consist of a blade or blades that can be adjusted to cut a dado, groove, or rabbet in a single pass. Dado heads are available with steel or carbide-tipped teeth. Because grooving doesn't

A stack dado head consists of two outside cutters, between which are sandwiched a number of chippers. Thin plastic, paper, or metal shims placed between the blades provide fine adjustment for the width of cut.

Dado Safety

Dado heads are dangerous. They remove a lot of wood in one pass, which increases the risk of kickback. In addition, cutting with a dado head requires removal of the splitter and antikickback fingers. Always use featherboards, hold-downs, push sticks, and a guard when working with a dado head.

normally require very deep cutting, a 6-in.-dia. or 8-in.-dia. dado head is usually sufficient for any shop. In general, use a dado head that is 2 in. less in diameter than the size of a saw's stock blade (e.g., an 8-in. dado head for a 10-in. saw). The arbor on some portable saws isn't long enough to accept a full $^{15}/_{16}$-in.-wide dado-head setup.

There are two basic types of dado heads: stack dadoes and wobble dadoes. A stack dado consists of two outer cutters, between which are sandwiched a number of chippers (see the photo above). The beveled teeth on the right-hand cutter "lean" to the right. The teeth on the left-hand cutter "lean" the other way, resulting in smoothly cut dado walls with minimal tearout. A cutter can have from 18 to 60 teeth. The chippers, which typically sport two, three, or four FTG teeth per blade, are designed to remove material quickly and leave a flat-bottom dado or groove.

A stack dado includes two ⅛-in.-wide cutters, a ¼-in.-wide chipper, a $^1/_{16}$-in.-wide chipper, and a few ⅛-in.-wide chippers. By using different combinations of chippers (or no chippers at all), you can adjust the overall width of the dado head to cut a dado or groove ranging from ¼ in. wide to $^{15}/_{16}$ in. wide in $^1/_{16}$-in. increments. You can fine-tune the width of the dado head using paper, plastic, or metal shims.

Another type of dado cutting tool is the adjustable dado head, known as the "wobble" or "drunken" dado head (see the top photo on p. 56).

Wobble dadoes that adjust on a hub provide an inexpensive alternative to stack dadoes. The V-dado on the right employs two blades.

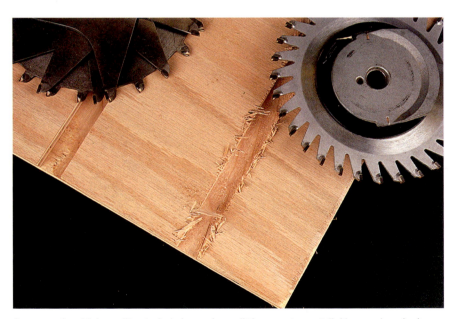

An expensive, high-quality stack dado produces little or no tearout (left), even in oak plywood. The ragged cut shown at right was made with an inexpensive wobble dado head.

With these tools, either one blade (wobble dado) or two blades (V-dado) are mounted on an adjustable hub at an angle, and the pitch of the blades can be adjusted for different-width grooves. (This is the ultimate example of blade runout.)

A premium-quality, top-of-the-line stack dado can cost close to $300. However, if your dadoes and grooves are mostly limited to jig making

Installing a Stack Dado Head

A STACK DADO HEAD CONSISTS OF TWO OUTSIDE CUTTERS, between which are sandwiched a number of chippers. After installing the right-hand cutter (typically marked as such), place a chipper against it with the chipper's teeth positioned within the cutter's gullets. Otherwise, you risk distorting the blades and damaging the teeth. Then install additional chippers and shims as necessary to build the dado out to the proper width. Space the teeth on each new chipper equally between the teeth on the previous chipper to prevent the dado head from running out of balance and stressing the arbor bearings (see the photo on p. 55). Last, install the second blade, again positioning the chipper teeth within the blade gullets.

Although you can buy a commercial dado-throat insert for your saw, it's best to make a custom "zero-clearance" throat plate that exactly accommodates the width of the dado head. That way, tearout will be minimized, even with a less-expensive dado set. Remember to clamp down the throat plate when raising the spinning head to cut your initial opening (see "Custom Throat Plates" on p. 99).

where rough cuts don't matter, you can get a wobble or V-dado for $100 or less. In my furniture making, I usually rout dadoes and grooves instead of sawing them. If I sawed a lot of dadoes, especially in plywood, I would buy a quality carbide stack dado for its ability to cut clean-walled, flat-bottom dadoes with minimal tearout (see the bottom photo on the facing page). Forrest makes a great stack dado for about $300 (see Sources on p. 197).

MOLDING HEADS

Molding cutters, which are used to shape stock, can be installed in a special head that mounts on the saw arbor (see the photo on p. 58). Like dado heads, molding heads are dangerous because they remove a lot of stock in one pass. In addition, the workpiece is often fed on edge, so guards have to be specially made to suit the job. Because of these reasons, I generally advise against using the table saw for this kind of shaping unless you use extraordinary safety precautions. Instead I recommend using a router table or shaper for most shaping work.

For the longest time, only two molding heads have been available—one made by Delta and one by Sears®. Neither have any features for safely limiting the depth of cut, which adds to the danger of kickback. Recently, though, a table-saw molding head has come on the market that is made in accordance with strict European safety regulations. Called the Magic Molder, the head has a chip-limiting design to reduce the chance of kickback, and the carbide cutters lock securely into a well-balanced aluminum head (see the photo on p. 58). If you want to use your table saw for shaping, the tool might be worth checking out (see Sources on p. 197).

A molding head can be mounted on a saw to shape profiles. The Magic Molder shown here limits the depth of cut to reduce the chance of kickback.

SCORING BLADES

A scoring blade is a small blade (about 4 in. in diameter) that makes a shallow cut ahead of the main sawblade. The scoring blade rotates in the opposite direction, making only a shallow, scoring cut to eliminate possible chipping or tearout from the main blade (see the photos on the facing page). Scoring blades are standard or optional equipment on most panel saws—saws with a built-in sliding table that are capable of handling a lot of sheet goods. At least one company—Modulus—has made an after-market scoring saw attachment that will fit most cabinet saws. The unit costs about $400 (see Sources on p. 197).

Blade Stiffeners

Flanged collars called blade stiffeners are precision-machined washers that help stabilize a running blade. Installed on the arbor next to the blade, they provide extra support to the blade, helping reduce vibration that can cause rough cutting and blade fatigue, particularly when using cheap or thin-kerf blades. Larger-diameter collars provide more support at the outer edges of the blade (see the photo on p. 60).

Typically, a single collar is installed on the outside of the blade, but you can also use two collars—one on the inside and one on the outside. However, placing a collar on the inside—next to the saw arbor's fixed collar—will reposition the blade on the arbor. This means you may have to make a throat plate to suit the new saw slot. You'll also have to readjust

Aftermarket scoring-blade assemblies can be retrofitted to most cabinet saws to eliminate tearout and chipping in plywood and other sheet goods.

The small scoring blade cuts a shallow kerf ahead of the main sawblade, eliminating tearout in fragile facing materials like oak plywood and melamine.

A blade stiffener mounted against the sawblade stabilizes it, reducing vibration and helping produce a cleaner cut.

the cursor on your fence-rail scale if you want to use it to set your rip fence (see "Custon Throat Plates" on p. 99).

Because using a blade stiffener also reduces the depth of cut, it's a good idea to note the blade's cutting capacity with the stiffener installed. You want to remember not to raise a spinning blade in the middle of a heavy cut, jamming the stiffener against a wooden throat plate and smoking up the shop as I have done.

Blade Care

A set of good sawblades can easily cost as much as some table saws, so it's a good idea to take care of your blades. Like other cutting tools, blades must be kept sharp and clean to perform at their best.

Keeping your blades sharp is important for reasons other than just getting clean cuts. Dull blades heat up while fighting their way through the wood. The heat causes gum and pitch buildup, which in turn increases the heat, often resulting in a warped blade. Working dull, hot blades can also lead to cracks in the plate, usually starting at the gullet. Regularly inspect your blades for cracks in the plate or chips in the teeth. Chipped teeth can be repaired by a saw smith, but a cracked blade should be discarded.

After softening and loosening pitch and resin on a blade using a cleaning solvent, scrub off the residue using a plastic- or brass-bristled brush. Oil the blade after cleaning.

Clean your blades regularly, especially when you're cutting resinous woods such as pine or cherry. Either paint remover (not paint thinner) or ammonia in warm water will often remove pitch and resins. Stay away from oven-cleaning products because they tend to break down the cobalt binder that holds the carbide particles together. A number of proprietary blade-cleaning products on the market these days do an excellent job of cleaning blades. I prefer a water-soluble, environmentally friendly cleaner because it's not as nasty to work with as many cleaners (see the photo above). After cleaning, blades should be dried thoroughly, then treated with a light coat of thin oil to prevent rust, particularly around the teeth.

You might think that because carbide is so hard it would be difficult to damage, but it's also very brittle and can crack and chip. Don't use a carbide blade to cut wood that may contain nails or other metal. And take care when handling and storing carbide-tipped blades. Never stack them directly against each other or lay them on the saw table; store them in an appropriate container.

Safety

According to an estimate by the U.S. Consumer Product Safety Commission, there was an average of more than 30,000 emergency-room admittances for table-saw-related hand injuries every year for the last 10 years. I believe it. Nearly every serious woodworker that I know has experienced at least one close call on the table saw. I myself remember being doubled over in front of my saw after getting slammed in

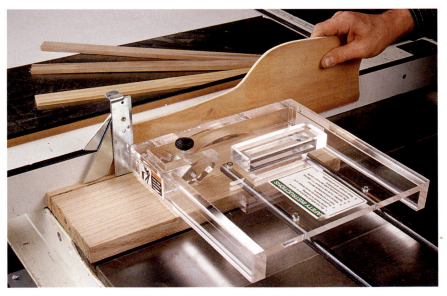

A blade guard and splitter or riving knife are essential table-saw accessories. Using a pusher to feed the wood keeps your hands out of harm's way.

Safety at the Table Saw

MANY ACCIDENTS AT THE TABLE SAW can be avoided by proper preparation and use of common sense. Your best safety precaution is a sharp mind. Concentrate on the task at hand and don't be distracted by conversation. Be aware that many accidents happen right after a large lunch, when you're often less alert.

Try to find the simplest way to make a cut; a fussy setup can invite problems. Use your common sense; if a setup seems dangerous, it probably is. Try a different approach or use a more appropriate tool. And take your time. Rushing is an all-too-common cause of accidents.

Dress Appropriately

Be aware that anything hanging or protruding near the blade can present a danger. Roll up loose sleeves, tuck in your shirt, tie back long hair, and doff any jewelry. Avoid gloves, even if it's cold, because they can catch on things and reduce your sensitivity. Wear shoes with non-skid soles, and avoid sandals. Keep your top pockets free of objects that could drop out onto the table.

Set Up for Safety

Make sure your saw is properly plugged into a grounded outlet because all that metal conducts electricity easily. Operate the saw only in a dry area. Always unplug the saw when changing blades or performing tune-ups, and make all adjustments with the blade at a dead stop. Set the blade no more than ¼ in. above the workpiece, and always double-check the rip fence to make sure it's locked in place before making a cut.

Keep Clean and Sharp

Keep the saw table free of tools, offcuts, and extra workpieces that could creep toward the blade. Use a dust brush instead of your hands to brush sawdust off the table. Use sharp, clean blades; they're less likely to kick back and will cut the work much easier. Resin-covered blades tend to build up heat and resist cutting. It's also wise to wash up after using the saw to minimize skin irritation from certain woods.

Use Proper Cutting Procedure

Use the rip fence for ripping and the miter gauge (or other appropriate jig) for crosscutting. Never cut freehand for any reason! And don't use the fence as a stop block for crosscutting; an offcut trapped between the fence and the blade can kick back violently.

Let the blade build up to full speed before cutting, then push the workpiece fully through the blade; stopping mid-cut invites kickback. Most important, stand to the side of the workpiece being cut. Always wait until the blade comes to a dead stop before picking up cut stock or clearing away offcuts.

the gut by a flying workpiece. I've also had cutoffs whiz by my head on their way to the other end of the shop. Fortunately, I escaped serious injury before learning proper safety techniques, but I know others who haven't been so lucky.

The good news is that table-saw accidents are almost entirely preventable—no exaggeration. In this chapter, I'll explain the causes of accidents and show you how to avoid them. I'll also discuss ways to protect your eyes, ears, and lungs as well as your limbs.

The Risks

Proper planning, dress, and saw setup can reduce many risks at the table saw (see the sidebar on p. 63). However, the three greatest potentials for table-saw harm involve the blade. The most prevalent accidents involve kickback, followed by ejection and laceration. All of these dangers can be eliminated by using the proper safety equipment and technique, as I'll discuss in the following sections.

KICKBACK

By far, the most common cause of table-saw accidents is kickback. Kickback is just the nature of the beast called the table saw. It's not necessarily the "fault" of the woodworker, the machine setup, or the workpiece; it's simply an inherent part of the cutting operation. Unless you're using a splitter or riving knife, kickback can occur even when the rip fence is set properly, the workpiece is flawless, and you're pushing correctly.

Kickback is caused by the tendency of the rising teeth at the rear of the blade to pick up the workpiece, catapulting it toward the operator at speeds approaching 100 miles per hour (see the sidebar on the facing page). As if the risk of getting smacked by the workpiece isn't bad enough, your hand can also be pulled toward the spinning blade in the process. And this all usually happens way too fast for you to pull yourself out of harm's way.

You can minimize the chance of kickback by adjusting your rip fence properly and holding the workpiece firmly against the fence for the entirety of the cut. But that's not the real solution. The only sure-fire way to prevent kickback is by using a properly adjusted splitter or riving knife, which denies the workpiece access to the blade's rear teeth. I'll discuss splitters and riving knives in more depth shortly.

EJECTION

Although a splitter or riving knife prevents kickback, a workpiece can still be ejected straight toward the front of the saw. This force is simply caused by the friction on the side of the rotating blade and is overcome by whatever feed force is being applied to the workpiece. The best protections against ejection are to push all pieces past the rear of the blade, not to cut pieces shorter than the distance between the front and back of the blade, and not to use the fence to crosscut.

You should also use a properly shaped push stick and feed the workpiece with a force and momentum appropriate for the size of and density of

Kickback Speed

A board that's kicked back by the sawblade can hurl a workpiece toward you at speeds approaching 100 miles per hour.

FOR AS OFTEN AS IT HAPPENS, KICKBACK IS NOT WELL UNDERSTOOD. For one thing, it occurs too quickly to observe. Here's what's actually taking place.

As a workpiece approaches the rear of the spinning blade, the rising rear teeth try to lift it upward. This is made worse by the fact that the sawn edge is always trying to press against the rear teeth due to the resistance at the front of the blade and the resistance from the pusher at the opposing diagonal corner. To understand the principle, lay a book on the table and plant a finger (representing the blade) on the table behind the far left-hand corner of the book. Then push the book forward from its right front corner (the pusher). Notice that the book pivots to the left, just as a workpiece pivots into the blade.

When ripping wood, one side of the workpiece is restrained against the fence, pinching the workpiece diagonally between the fence and blade. The workpiece then rides up on top of the spinning blade and is hurled backward and to the left toward the operator at speeds up to 100 miles per hour. The workpiece is typically left with a scar in the shape of an arc as evidence of its rough ride over the top of the blade.

The only way to entirely eliminate kickback is to use a properly aligned splitter or riving knife (see "Aligning the Splitter to the Blade" on p. 105). If you insist on working without a splitter or riving knife (I won't!), you can at least minimize the chances of kickback by taking the following measures, although they aren't foolproof: Keep the workpiece firmly against the fence for the entirety of the cut. A shoe-type pusher with a long sole will help you provide some side pressure (see "Pushers" on p. 79).

Be particularly careful when trimming square pieces, which are prone to creeping away from the fence. If the workpiece edge that's bearing against the fence is shorter than the adjacent edges, use a miter gauge or crosscut sled instead of the fence to guide the workpiece.

As a workpiece strays from the fence, it can become diagonally pinched between the blade and the rip fence, inviting kickback.

As the workpiece is lifted by the rising rear teeth of the blade, it climbs over the top of the blade, traveling backward.

The workpiece is hurtled diagonally backward toward the operator.

The arched scar on the underside of the workpiece is a result of its travel over the top of the blade.

the wood. Don't let the heel of a push stick ride up over the end of the workpiece. Some splitters include notched pawls or "fingers" intended to prevent ejection, but I've found them to be very unreliable.

LACERATION

Any part of an exposed blade presents a danger to flesh and bone. The best protection is a blade cover, often called a blade guard. A cover prevents your hands from accidentally coming in contact with the blade. It also prevents sawdust and splinters from being thrown at the operator. Many lacerations occur while removing cutoffs from the table before the blade (even a covered blade) has stopped. It's a good habit to lower an uncovered blade below the table when you're finished cutting. Even a stopped blade can hurt you.

Although many woodworkers remove the troublesome stock blade cover that came with their saws, a number of well-designed aftermarket blade covers are available as replacements. There are also other creative ways to cover the blade for specific cutting operations, as discussed in chapters 7–9.

Safety Accessories

The essential safety equipment for any table-saw operation includes a good splitter or riving knife and a blade cover. Other accessories such as pushers, auxiliary workpiece supports, featherboards, safety wheels, and power feeders also have their particular uses.

STOCK BLADE GUARDS

The stock table-saw guard systems on most saws sold in the United States are awful. There, somebody has said it. Nearly every woodworker knows this, even though woodworking experts insist in books, magazines, and television shows that we use our table-saw guards. They tell us that *they* have removed the guards on *their* table saws only so we can better see the operation they're performing. Nonsense. The reason why they and so many other woodworkers discard stock guards is that the guards are poorly designed for their purpose.

A stock blade guard is actually a three-in-one system that is bolted to the saw's carriage assembly. The system combines a splitter, a blade cover, and antikickback fingers in one assembly (see the top photo on p. 40). Unfortunately, this design approach severely limits the usefulness of the system. First, because the splitter is fixed in place and stands higher than the blade, only through saw cuts can be made. To cut dadoes, grooves, rabbets, and many other joints, the entire guard assembly must be unbolted from the saw—not a quick and easy operation.

The splitter also prevents use of crosscut sleds and other jigs. To make matters worse, the blade cover on many assemblies won't stay up and out of the way for blade changing or measuring sawblade height. Ultimately, because removing and reattaching the guard assembly is such a pain, it is often cast aside in a dark corner of the shop to collect dust.

That said, these guard systems are better than nothing at all. They do work; they're just terribly inconvenient. Even so, I would use one rather than nothing at all. However, read on for better alternatives to stock guards.

SPLITTERS AND RIVING KNIVES

A splitter or riving knife is the most important piece of safety equipment for a table saw because it virtually eliminates the potential for kickback—the most common table-saw accident. As I've explained, a splitter or riving knife denies access to the upward rising teeth at the rear of a sawblade, preventing a workpiece from being thrown.

A riving knife, which is attached to the blade-arbor assembly, is a much better solution than a typical splitter, which doesn't rise and fall with the blade. Sadly, riving knives are only available on European saws. Curved in shape, a riving knife sits about ¼ in. behind the blade and a little below the blade height (see the photo below). Therefore, it does not get in the way of any cut or jig that a woodworker normally uses. The only reason to change it would be to install a smaller- or larger-diameter blade.

The fact that the riving knife sits so closely behind the blade ensures that the workpiece is held away from the rear teeth almost immediately after the workpiece passes the blade. Unfortunately, these proprietary splitters cannot be retrofit to a different saw.

Riving Knives

Although the terms splitter and riving knife are sometimes used interchangeably, a splitter typically refers to a plate attached to the rear of the saw or to the throat plate. With the exception of the Delta Disappearing Splitter, a splitter cannot be adjusted in height. A riving knife, typically on European saws, is fixed to the blade-arbor assembly, so it always moves relative to the blade and stays in proper position, regardless of blade height or tilt.

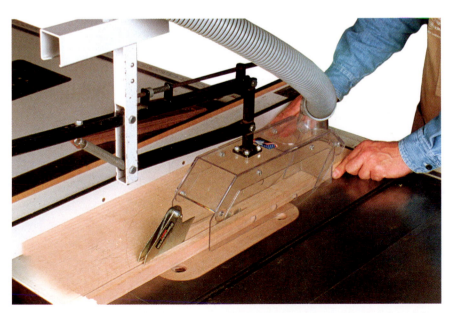

The riving knife on a typical European saw is attached to the arbor carriage and rises, falls, and tilts with the blade.

The Delta Disappearing Splitter can be pushed down under the throat plate for non-through-cutting operations such as grooving and rabbeting.

A Shopmade Splitter

As DISCUSSED IN THE SIDEBAR on p. 99, a zero-clearance throat plate has many advantages over the stock throat plate that comes with your saw. In addition, it's easy to create a shopmade splitter by simply gluing a piece of hardwood or other thin material into the blade slot of a zero-clearance throat plate (see photo below).

A splitter is most effective when placed close to the rear of the blade. Because the blade progresses toward the rear of the throat plate as it's raised for thicker cuts, make at least two throat plates—one for cutting stock up to about 1 in. thick and another for thicker stock. To make a throat plate for thick stock, you'll need to elongate the slot by flipping the throat plate end for end, then raising the blade. This allows you to place the splitter farther back.

It's important to align the right side of the splitter with the right-hand side of the blade teeth. To fine-tune the position of the splitter, install a short screw in the end or side of the throat plate to take up any play in its fit. The insert can also be sanded if necessary to reduce its thickness.

A piece of hardwood glued into the slot in a zero-clearance throat plate serves as a shopmade splitter.

The best alternative—short of buying a European saw—is to get an aftermarket splitter designed to fit saws manufactured for the U.S. market. There are currently four models available: two made by Delta, one by Biesemeyer, and one by Excalibur. The other alternative is to make your own splitter (see the sidebar above).

Unlike the splitter on the stock three-in-one system, aftermarket splitters can all be removed and reinstalled easily. Because they all install on the rear of the carriage assembly, some space remains between the blade and the splitter, especially when the blade is set low. Although this allows some potential for kickback, it's very small.

The Delta Disappearing Splitter The Delta Disappearing Splitter is the oldest splitter and the one with which I have had the most experience. It was designed to fit the right-tilting Delta UniSaw® as part of Delta's original UniGuard® system. Although the original UniGuard has been discontinued in favor of the Deluxe UniGuard, the Disappearing Splitter is still available.

This splitter is not removable from its holder. Instead, it can be pushed down below the table into its holder when not needed (see the photo on the facing page). To raise the splitter, you need only remove the throat plate and pull the splitter up, at which point it automatically locks in place. Being nonremovable, it is always at hand and easy to bring into play. Because the Disappearing Splitter is thin and narrow, it will work with thin-kerf blades as well as standard blades. However, the thin metal is also easily bent, calling for caution when handling large or heavy workpieces.

The Delta Disappearing Splitter costs about $100 and will mount only on the right-tilting Unisaw and right-tilting Jet cabinet saw.

The Delta Deluxe UniGuard Splitter This newer model splitter from Delta is clamped to its holder with a knurled, threaded knob, which is unscrewed to remove the splitter (see the photo at right). As with the Delta Disappearing Splitter, the UniGuard Splitter may also be used with thin-kerf blades. Because the UniGuard Splitter is wider than the Disappearing Splitter, it is not as prone to bending, although it's not as sturdy as the Biesemeyer splitter.

The Delta Deluxe UniGuard Splitter costs about $30 and will fit all of Delta's table saws including the left-tilting UniSaw, except the portable saws. It should also fit Jet cabinet saws.

The Biesemeyer Splitter The Biesemeyer splitter is a solid ⅛-in.-thick piece of steel that sits in a heavy-duty holder (see the photo below). The splitter can be snapped into its holder without removing the saw's throat

The Delta Deluxe UniGuard Splitter is clamped in place with a threaded knob, which also allows you to remove it for non-through-cutting operations.

The Biesemeyer splitter snaps easily into its mounting bracket and can be removed by retracting the round knob on the bracket.

Use a Splitter

Although the blade cover does protect against laceration, it does *not* prevent kickback. Only a splitter or riving knife will do that. Don't be lulled into a false sense of security that a covered blade might imply!

The rear of the Excalibur splitter hooks over a rear-mount assembly, while the front end clicks into a mount inside the saw on the blade carriage.

plate. Removal, however, does require getting under the throat plate to retract a spring-loaded rod on the holder. To avoid having to remove the throat plate to access the knob, I drilled a 1-in.-dia. hole in my saw's throat plate that allows insertion of a stick for pulling the knob. This splitter is very sturdy and cannot be easily bent. While contributing to solidity and durability, the ⅛-in. thickness prevents use of the splitter when working with thin-kerf blades.

Biesemeyer splitters cost about $120 and are currently available for all models of Delta saws except portables. They will also fit Powermatic® saws, General® saws, and Jet saws.

The Excalibur Merlin Splitter The Merlin splitter is a bit different from other aftermarket splitters in that it attaches to the rear of a table saw rather than to the rear of the carriage assembly (see the photo above). It's easy to remove and replace and should fit many of the most common tables saws including Craftsman®. I haven't tried it yet, as it was still in development as of this writing.

BETTER BLADE COVERS

As an alternative to stock blade-guard systems, there are currently five overhead blade-cover systems available, sold either as part of a saw package or as an aftermarket accessory. An overhead cover is independent of a saw's splitter or riving knife, allowing non-through-cutting operations to be covered when the splitter or riving knife has been removed. Four of the five aftermarket cover systems also include dust-collection ports, creating a somewhat healthier work environment.

Delta Deluxe Blade Guard.

An overhead cover can be adjusted horizontally to accommodate a tilted blade or to minimize the space between the cover and the fence for easier ripping of narrow pieces. When crosscutting, the side of the cover can be adjusted close to the blade to prevent trapping short cutoffs between the blade and side of the cover. For cutting tall pieces, the cover can be moved entirely away from the blade. All of the systems are removable for those rare occasions when oversized work requires an unusual amount of free space around the blade.

Delta Deluxe Blade Guard The supporting frame of the Delta is a C-shaped piece of hollow tubing, the bottom arm of which is bracketed to the rear of the saw and to the rear edge of the side extension table. The upper arm is a telescoping boom that supports a two-piece basket-style blade cover (see the photo above). A plastic tray mounted on the upper arm will hold a note pad, tape measure, push stick, and a slot to store a removable splitter.

The Delta's split blade cover is an innovative design, providing extra safety in some cutting situations. For example, after crosscutting thick stock, half of the cover drops down for protection even though the cutoff holds half of the cover up above the spinning blade. The cover is sloped at the front to ride up easily onto an approaching workpiece. Stop collars on the arm allow the halves of the cover to flip up out of the way for changing blades and setting up cuts. There is no dust-collection port on the cover.

Although the top arm of the C-frame is only 10 in. above the table, there is still enough access for pushers and crosscut sleds without feeling cramped. The telescoping arm allows for very little movement to the right of the blade, but the arm can easily be removed if it obstructs cutting tall, wide workpieces. Rotating the extended section moves the blade cover forward and backward in relation to the blade. For cutting very long and wide boards, the whole frame can be swung below the work surface by loosening one bolt on each of the frame brackets. However, a rear outfeed table that is wider than 36 in. from the left side of the saw will prevent the arm from swinging down.

This guard is designed for Delta table saws and fence systems. It will not work with fence systems that require use of a rear rail for fence operation. On Biesemeyer-style fence systems, the rear rail is used only to support a side table, and the rail can be replaced with Delta's flat metal bar. Although a flat bar doesn't provide a ledge for supporting a rear outfeed table, a freestanding table could be used.

If budget is a consideration and you have a Delta table saw, the Delta Deluxe Blade Guard is the best buy of all these systems. Considering that it includes a splitter, this package might fit your equipment budget. The lack of a dust-collection port is a disadvantage, but it may be outweighed by the cost savings compared with other models.

Biesemeyer T-Square Blade Guard System Like the Delta, the Biesemeyer support frame is C-shaped. The lower arm of the rectangular tubing mounts with a couple of bolts and screws to the L-shaped rear rail of a Biesemeyer-style fence system. The telescoping upper arm supports a basket-style cover that can accept an optional dust-collection port (see the photo below). A perpendicular channel at the end of the arm allows easy fore-and-aft adjustment of the cover, as well as its removal.

A counterbalanced mechanism allows the cover to self-adjust to suit any thickness of workpiece while staying parallel to the saw table. When

Biesemeyer T-Square Blade Guard System.

lifted all the way up, the cover locks into place about 7 in. above the table. The cover can be moved well to the right of the blade for using tall jigs or cutting vertically supported workpieces. The telescoping movement is controlled by an internal threaded rod connected to an adjusting crank on the far end of the upper arm.

A release lever allows for quick, gross adjustments of the arm, but I still found this somewhat cumbersome. To overcome the problem, I removed the threaded rod altogether, allowing for quick, easy adjustments made from my normal working position.

Because the post mounts to the rear of the extension table, you can crosscut any length workpiece up to 12 in. wide before it is stopped by the post. For easy removal of the entire system, I attached it to the rear fence rail with 3-in.-wide plastic wing nuts. Alternative mountings include a bolt-down floor stand or a ceiling mount.

The Biesemeyer is one of my favorite systems because of its overall ease of use and relative unobtrusiveness. It's only real disadvantage is its inability to be used on saws that require a rear rail for fence operation.

Excalibur Overarm Blade Cover The Excalibur consists of a square post that supports a round, hollow, telescoping arm to which the blade cover is connected (see the photo below). The two-piece post is bolted to the end of the extension table rather than to its rear edge. This means the Excalibur can be used with any fence system since it won't interfere with rear fence rails. The lower section of the post extends to the floor and is held upright by two metal braces that connect to the extension table. The upper section of the post slides into the lower section, locking in place with a lever, which allows you to easily remove the entire upper section of the system if necessary.

Dust-Collection Aid

Some aftermarket blade covers incorporate a dust-collection port for evacuating much of the sawdust thrown upward by the blade.

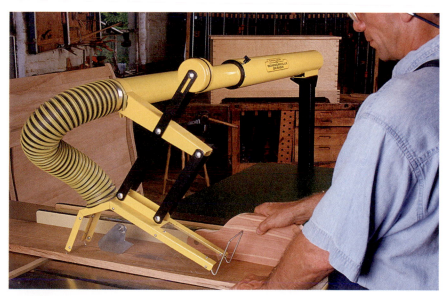

Excalibur Overarm Blade Cover.

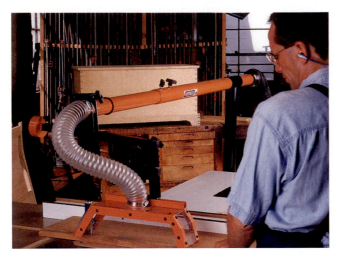

Exaktor Industrial Overarm Blade Cover.

Brett-Guard Cantilever Mount.

The basket-style blade cover can be locked in place at any height up to 8 in. above the table. A lever allows you to lock the cover down onto a workpiece for safer cutting of thin stock and dadoes. A wire handle at the front of the blade cover offers a safe, convenient grasp of the cover and allows the cover to ramp up onto approaching stock. The rear plastic panel can be removed to accommodate a stock or aftermarket splitter. The cover can be moved fairly easily 24 in. to the right of the blade.

For dust collection, a length of hose connects the blade cover to one end of the upper arm. A 4-in.-dia. dust-collector hose connects to the opposite end of the arm. The whole arm is sealed for optimum vacuum efficiency.

The Excalibur offers sturdy quality and superior dust collection. However, the unit is heavy and places a lot of weight at the end of the extension table, which can cause the table to twist, so this system may not be the best choice for a saw mounted on a mobile base.

Exaktor Industrial Overarm Blade Cover The Exaktor consists of a two-piece round post that supports a round, hollow, telescoping arm that carries a basket-style blade cover. Like the Excalibur, the post attaches to the end of the extension table so it won't interfere with any fence system (see the photo at left above). The lower section of the post can be bolted to the floor for a sturdy installation. The post is further stabilized by means of a turnbuckle extending from the bottom section of the post to the underside of the extension table. The upper section of the post (along with the telescoping arm) can be lifted completely out of the lower section after releasing a locking handle on the post. The arm can also simply pivot out of the way in its post.

The cover assembly lifts easily out of the way for setting up cuts and can be locked at any height. A dust port on the cover connects via a hose to the hollow telescoping arm. A rubber collar at the opposite end of the arm adapts to fit a standard 4-in.-dia. dust-collector hose. The dust-collection system works great. Unfortunately, the blunt front end of the cover does not allow an approaching workpiece to slide under it. You must either lift the blade cover onto the work or lock it to hover above the workpiece.

The cover will slide well to the right of the blade by pushing the telescoping arm to the right. However, it takes two hands to lift and push the arm because the fit is a bit rough. Also, the lack of a registry channel between the two pieces of the arm allows the inner arm to rotate when unlocked. This can cause the blade cover to move out of parallel to the table surface or workpiece. In its favor, the arm sits about 19 in. above the table surface, allowing plenty of unrestricted space to work.

The rear of the cover includes two slots to accommodate a splitter. The unused slot is covered when not in use. Unfortunately, with a splitter installed you are not able to adjust the cover horizontally for finer adjustments—for example, when ripping narrow pieces.

The Exaktor is less expensive than most of the other models and is sufficient as a blade cover, but it lacks the sturdiness of the Excalibur and the lightweight efficiency of the Biesemeyer. Because the Exaktor mounts on the floor, it also lacks mobility. It is, however, a very efficient collector of dust at the blade, and you can purchase the blade-cover assembly separately for ceiling mounting or other custom installations.

Brett-Guard® Cantilever Mount The C-shaped frame on the Brett-Guard Cantilever Mount guard screws to a rear support angle, which is not needed if the table saw already has a Biesemeyer-style rear fence rail. Fence systems that require a rear rail for fence operation can still be used with this system. The blade cover is connected by a bracket to a control housing that is hinged to a platform on the end of the upper arm (see the photo at right on the facing page).

The Brett differs from the other blade covers in that it does not use a basket-style cover. Instead, a clear, thick, plastic box that provides great visibility connects to a control housing that the user adjusts manually. The underside of one edge of the cover is scalloped, so the blade can be set right at the edge of the cover for ripping narrow stock (see the photo on p. 62).

The cover height is adjusted using a crank on top of the housing. Unlike typical gravity-controlled covers, all adjustments are positive; the cover does not lift or drop on its own. Adjusting the cover to hold down a workpiece helps reduce kickback. (The cover includes an antikickback device, but I couldn't get it to work properly no matter what.) Of course, when the cover is fixed at the height of a thick workpiece, the blade is somewhat exposed after the cut. Although the cover comes with a dust port, you must provide your own hose and fittings.

The SawStop™

TABLE-SAW SAFETY IS IN FOR A REAL SHAKE-UP. A recent invention called the SawStop promises to revolutionize saw safety by stopping the blade upon contact with skin. The device consists of a heavy-duty, spring-loaded, replaceable brake pawl that slams into the blade, stopping it within one-quarter of a turn and causing it to drop immediately below the table. This action takes place in a few milliseconds, turning what could have been an amputation into just a minor cut.

The SawStop works by sensing the electrical conductivity of your body. When your skin touches the blade, it affects a fuse in the device that releases the brake. Cutting wet wood doesn't trigger the brake, although metal will. Before cutting aluminum, brass, or other soft metals that can be cut on a table saw, you'll need to turn off the SawStop.

Unfortunately, the SawStop cannot be retrofit to existing saws and, in fact, calls for an internal redesign of existing saws. Although it's not in production at the time of this writing, there's little doubt that the SawStop will become an integral part of table saws produced within the next few years.

As great an invention as it is, the SawStop is really a second line of defense on the table saw and protects only against laceration. It won't protect against kickback, which is the most common accident at the saw. To prevent against kickback, you need to use a properly aligned splitter or riving knife, as discussed on pp. 67–70. That said, saws of the future that include a European-style riving knife as well as a blade brake like the SawStop will be a welcome addition indeed to any woodshop.

The cover can easily be flipped up out of the way for setting up a cut. It can also be moved 20 in. to the right of the blade when necessary, although the heavy control housing requires using a bit of force to slide the upper arm. When the arm is slid over fully and the housing and blade cover are flipped up out of the way, there is plenty of access for a crosscut box or tall workpieces.

Unfortunately, the Brett allows little accommodation for an after-market splitter. A splitter has to sit outside of and behind this cover. After adjusting the cover forward, I was still only able to use the narrow Delta UniSaw Disappearing Splitter. The Brett comes with its own splitter, but it bolts in place just like a stock table-saw splitter and is just as inconvenient. This cover really calls for a shopmade splitter in the throat plate.

Brett-Guard Original Mount   Like the cover on the Brett-Guard Cantiliver Mount, the cover on the Original Mount is a heavy-duty, square plastic box that provides great visibility of the blade. However, this model is suspended on two metal rods that attach to a platform that mounts on your saw's left or right extension wing (see the photo on the facing page).

The guard is easily removed and reattached and can be slid out of the way for blade setups. An adjustment crank on the platform raises and low-

Brett-Guard Original Mount.

ers the cover, which is meant to ride lightly on top of the workpiece. You can adjust it to hover above the blade right next to the rip fence, making it ideal for ripping narrow pieces (see the photo on p. 62). Because the unit attaches to the saw table, your cutting capacity is limited to the distance between the cover and its platform.

Like the Brett-Guard Cantilever Mount, this table-mounted version allows little accommodation for an aftermarket splitter, although the Delta Disappearing Splitter is small enough to use. Alternatively, you could use a shopmade splitter.

FEATHERBOARDS AND SAFETY WHEELS

Featherboards and safety wheels are shopmade or commercial hold-down devices that prevent kickback by holding workpieces firmly against the table or fence, allowing you to keep you hands away from the blade. As helpful as they are, these devices are not intended to be a line of first defense against kickback. To prevent kickback, you really need a splitter or riving knife. However, featherboards and safety wheels can help during operations when using a splitter or riving knife is difficult or impossible.

Featherboards, or fingerboards, are wood, metal, or plastic accessories that clamp in the miter-gauge slot or to the table to prevent the workpiece from moving backward from the blade toward the operator (see the top photo on p. 78).

Although featherboards are available commercially, it's easy to make your own (see the sidebar on the facing page).

Safety wheels consist of a pair of wheels that mount directly on the rip fence or on an auxiliary fence. The wheels adjust for various thicknesses of materials and, when set properly, hold the workpiece against the fence and

A featherboard applies springlike pressure to hold a workpiece against the fence or table, preventing backward travel at the same time.

Pushers can be bought or made in various shapes to suit particular ripping tasks.

table. One-way bearings prevent backward rotation. Many woodworkers who use safety wheels find them most beneficial when cutting sheet goods or other large panels and when cutting grooves and rabbets.

Although safety wheels seem to be a popular substitute for a missing guard assembly, I find them somewhat obstructive. In many cases, you have to either use a low push stick to push the workpiece under the wheels or else pull the stock out from the rear of the saw. Of course, with a splitter or riving knife, guard, and antikickback fingers in place, the wheels aren't necessary for most operations.

Shopmade Featherboards

A FEATHERBOARD CAN BE MADE FROM ANY CLEAR, fairly straight-grained scrap wood. Depending on the application, you can use either 4/4 or 8/4 stock. About the only time I use featherboards at the table saw is for edge grooving or rabbeting, which are both cases where a thicker featherboard works better. For edge grooving, the thicker featherboard helps steady the vertical workpiece while holding it flat against the fence. When rabbeting, a wide, thick featherboard acts as a blade cover while holding the work down on the table.

To make a featherboard, select a scrap 3 in. to 6 in. wide and long enough to overhang the left edge of the saw table for clamping purposes. Mark a line across the board about 6 in. from the end and cut that end off at about 30 degrees. Using a bandsaw or a jigsaw, make a series of parallel cuts ⅛ in. to ¼ in. apart from the angled end of the board. This will make the flexible feathers that allow the work to be fed in only one direction.

Pushstick Design

The ideal pusher is one that keeps your hand well above the fence and that provides pressure over a good length of the workpiece. A comfortable wooden pusher will have no sharp edges.

The long sole on a shoe-type pusher provides great bearing and control when ripping.

Pushers Pushers are used as extensions of your hands to push the work through the sawblade. Made of wood or plastic, they are an important piece of safety equipment to help protect your fingers. A well-designed pusher will also provide good control of the workpiece. Like many accessories, pushers are available commercially, but you can also easily make them yourself in many shapes, sizes, and styles (see the bottom photo on the facing page).

The pushers I use the most are shaped like a shoe, with a long sole, a toe, and a heel. The long sole and heel work in combination to hold the work to the table and against the fence (see the photo above). The length and height of the toe can be varied to negotiate tight places. For example, a long, narrow toe will fit under antikickback fingers when ripping very narrow workpieces. I bandsaw my own pushers from scrap wood, making them tall enough to keep my hand above the fence. My pushers range from ⅛ in. to 2 in. thick—I use a ¾-in.-thick pusher the most.

Power feeders For production sawing, a power feeder attached to the saw can be a good option. The motor-driven wheels on these units feed the work automatically into the sawblade. This pretty much eliminates any danger when ripping, since your hands are nowhere near the blade. Power feeders are expensive though, ranging from about $350 to more than $1,500.

Outfeed supports Auxiliary outfeed supports for the table saw are more than a convenience; they're an important safety addition. Without outfeed support, even the shortest pieces of wood will fall off the table at the end of a cut. To prevent them from falling, you would have to reach over the spinning blade to retrieve them—a very dangerous move, even with a guard. Although an outfeed roller can help, it doesn't provide a flat surface to carry the workpiece. An extension table is a much better solution, even if it extends only 18 in. behind the saw (see "Auxiliary Supports" on p. 119).

HEARING PROTECTION

The table saw is a loud machine, and prolonged exposure to the noise can subtly but permanently damage your hearing. Noise is measured in terms of decibels. Hearing loss begins with prolonged exposure to noise above 85 decibels, and a table saw typically operates at about 100 decibels. Do the math: Use ear protection. It's also a good idea to have your hearing examined periodically to keep tabs on your hearing health.

Hearing protectors are the main line of defense against noise-induced hearing loss. When investigating hearing protectors, compare noise-reduction ratings (NRR). The NRR is the amount of noise, measured in decibels, that a protector blocks out. Acceptable hearing protectors for the table saw should have an NRR of at least 25.

Safety gear is worthless if inconvenience deters you from using it, so get hearing protectors that are comfortable and convenient. There are three types of hearing protectors: hearing bands, earmuffs, and ear inserts (see the photo on the facing page). The first two are the types I use most frequently.

Hearing bands Hearing bands are my favorite type of ear protection. They are lightweight, plastic bands that fit under the chin or behind the head and don't interfere with wearing glasses. Because hearing bands are very lightweight, you can comfortably carry them around your neck so they're right at hand when needed. Plastic or foam pads at the ends of the band fit into or over the ear canal. I prefer soft foam pads to plastic cones. The cones are made to fit into any size ear canal, but after a while, I feel as though they're painfully widening my canals. Hearing bands cost less than $10 and are available through woodworking or safety-supply catalogs.

Hire an Electrician

If you're at all uncertain about electrical matters, hire a competent licensed electrician to do any wiring you need in your shop.

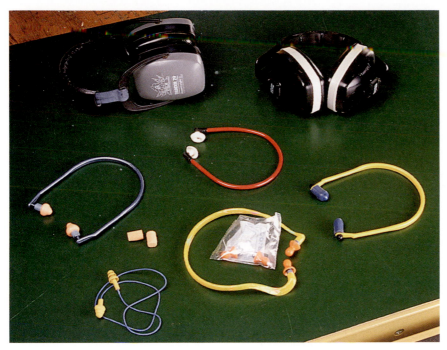

Earmuffs, hearing bands, and ear inserts are available in a wide range of styles, materials, and colors.

Earmuffs I also use full-sized earmuffs to protect my ears from machine noise. The first set of earmuffs I bought were heavy and uncomfortable, and I didn't like wearing them. The ones I use now are lightweight and more comfortable, so I'll wear them for longer periods of time. The main reason I don't use earmuffs as much as hearing bands is that muffs feel like they're choking me when I carry them around my neck. And if I set them down, they never seem to be at hand when I need them. (If you prefer earmuffs, belt loops are available for them.) When wearing muffs, be careful that glasses or spectacles don't break the seal around the ear. Any air that gets to the ear will carry sound, reducing the effectiveness of the muffs.

Ear inserts Ear inserts are small cylinders, typically made of foam, that expand inside the ear canal to block out noise. They are inexpensive and comfortable to wear, but my invariably dusty hands soil them quickly, so I tend not to use them.

EYE SAFETY
In my early days as a woodworker, I didn't give a lot of thought to eye protection. I wore regular prescription glasses, used a blade cover, and had dust collection hooked up to my saw. I figured I was pretty well protected. Eventually, though, I learned that regular prescription glasses aren't designed to withstand a heavy impact. Even with a blade guard and dust collector, you're still susceptible to eye injuries ranging from sawdust in the eye to serious puncture wounds requiring immediate medical attention.

Safety spectacles provide cheap and effective eye protection for most sawing tasks. Goggles (right) wrap fully around the eyes for maximum protection during particularly dusty tasks.

Set Your Speed Dial

If your shop phone has speed-dial capability, it's wise to dedicate a button or two for emergency dialing of your local fire or ambulance service.

These days, there's a great variety of safety eyewear available (see the photo above). You can get everything from basic frames to wraparound designer frames with tinted lenses and adjustable temples. Accessories like ear pads, elastic holders, and safety cords make safety glasses more comfortable and convenient than ever. And they're relatively cheap—starting at about $2. Choices of safety eyewear include safety spectacles, safety prescription glasses, and goggles.

Safety spectacles Safety spectacles approved by the American National Standards Institute (ANSI) are antifog, antiscratch, and antistatic. They are moderately impact-resistant but not unbreakable. Whenever there is a danger of severe impact, it's a good idea to wear a face shield in addition to safety spectacles.

Safety prescription glasses I have been using scratch-resistant safety lenses in my prescription glasses for quite a while. (Contact lenses aren't suitable for a dusty shop environment.) Safety prescription lenses are available for regular, bifocal, or multifocal lenses. When you order safety prescription lenses, be sure to specify polycarbonate for high-impact resistance. Prescription safety lenses aren't as protective as regular safety glasses because they typically lack top and side shields, but these are sometimes available as options.

Goggles Goggles—which wrap totally around the eyes—provide the kind of protection that is needed when performing dust-intensive tasks such as cutting coves or finger joints. I used to avoid wearing goggles at any cost because they were so uncomfortable and scratched so easily. Today, much better quality goggles are available, and I have a good comfortable pair that is fog- and scratch-resistant.

First-Aid for Eye Injuries

IT'S IMPORTANT TO KNOW HOW TO DEAL WITH EYE INJURIES in the woodshop. Eye injuries can range from irritating to painful to sight threatening. The most common injuries involve small particles of dust. If these are not removed by normal tear flow, they can usually be flushed out with clean water running over an open eye. An eye cup, available at pharmacies, can also be used to flood the eye.

Often, a small particle that is stuck under the upper eyelid can be removed by pulling the upper lid down over the lower lid. In the process, the eyelashes of the lower lid wipe the inner surface of the upper lid to dislodge the particle.

To remove particles from the lower lid, you can pull the lid down to expose the inner surface, then lift the particle with a sterile piece of gauze. Never try to lift a particle with a sharp object such as the tip of a knife. Try to resist the urge to rub your eyes; you can scratch your eye or drive a particle deeper into it. Once a particle is removed, it may still feel like something is in there. If pain persists, seek medical attention. Sometimes particles may be virtually invisible but can be detected by using a dye administered by a medical professional.

If you're not wearing safety eyewear, small chips or splinters thrown by the blade can stick in the eye or, worse yet, puncture it. Never try to remove these yourself. Instead, cover the eye with a bandage compress and have someone take you to a doctor. If you're alone, call an ambulance.

If you get smacked in the eye with a piece of wood, a cold compress will alleviate the pain and swelling. If you feel pain inside the eye or experience blurred or double vision, get medical help as soon as possible. Blood under the cornea is usually a sign of a cut eye. Seek medical attention immediately. Don't rub the eye—putting pressure on a cut eye can force out the inner fluid or even the retina, resulting in partial or total blindness. Protect a cut eye by covering it with a sterile bandage. A piece of cardboard or other stiff material placed over the bandage will protect the eye from pressure.

Don't treat eye injuries lightly. It's better to get professional medical attention immediately than to risk possible loss of sight.

Dust Protection

Although the table saw doesn't produce the volume of dust that a sander does, it's enough to cause a health hazard. Exposure to dust from wood and composition materials has been associated with skin and eye irritation, allergic reactions, asthma, nasal cancer, colon cancer, and salivary gland cancer, among other illnesses. The dusts of certain woods may be especially irritating to some woodworkers. And wood dust doesn't have to be noticeably irritating to be doing damage to your system.

Wood dust spewn from a saw can be hazardous in other ways too. It's slippery, and a sawdust-covered floor in front of the table saw can be a danger when ripping, which requires sure-footedness. (A nonskid mat in front of the saw can help with this.)

DUST MANAGEMENT AT THE SAW

There are a number of ways to reduce the amount of dust produced by your saw. For one, keep your blades sharp; sharp blades make shavings, whereas dull blades make dust. A second way is to use a blade cover, which will deflect dust and shavings downward onto the table instead of at you. Of course, this also helps protect your eyes, skin, and lungs. Third, you can install a dust-collection system, as discussed on p. 114.

DUST MASKS

Over the years, I've been dissatisfied with most of the dust masks I've tried. Most of them are uncomfortable, fit poorly, and cause my glasses to fog up. I eventually found two types of masks that I can tolerate: a soft silicone half-mask, and a double-strap paper face mask (see the photo below). The silicone half-mask fits tightly over the face and has a one-way valve for exhalation to reduce moisture collection in the mask. You inhale through replaceable dust filters. This mask can also be fitted with organic vapor filters for protection against chemicals in finishes and strippers. I use these masks for prolonged sanding and other heavy dust protection.

Double-strap dust masks are approved for lower dust concentrations. They are disposable and cost less than $1 each. I use these masks for short bouts with sawdust and to outfit occasional helpers. Don't confuse the double-strap masks with the more common single-strap masks, which are thinner, ill fitting, and not safety approved.

Half-masks with replaceable filters serve well for extended sawing and sanding operations. Double-strap paper masks provide adequate protection for brief bouts with dust.

First-Aid Procedures

Woodworkers should become familiar with basic first-aid procedures for removing splinters, dealing with eye injuries (see the sidebar on p. 83), and controlling bleeding. The best way to educate yourself about these procedures is to add a first-aid guide to your shop library. Standard references include *The AMA Handbook of First Aid and Emergency Care* (Random House®, 1990) and *First Aid Guide* (National Safety Council, 1991).

It's also critical to know what to do in the event of severe hand lacerations or amputated fingers, which unfortunately are not uncommon occurrences at the table saw. I asked a local hand surgeon for a list of recommended procedures for dealing with serious hand injuries, and I strongly advise you to do the same.

Every workshop should have a well-equipped first-aid kit in a convenient location (see the photo below). A fire extinguisher is another essential piece of safety equipment. Keep the phone numbers of your doctor, hospital, and ambulance service in plain view at the phone, and make sure you know the fastest route to the hospital. If you have a programmable phone, one-button emergency dialing can save your life.

First-Aid Kit
A basic first-aid kit for the shop should include the following: • sharp tweezers • scissors • adhesive tape • 2-in. by 2-in. and 3-in. by 3-in. sterile pads • 1-in. by 3-in. sterile bandages • antiseptic wipes • antiseptic ointment • instant cold compress • mild pain reliever • plastic gloves

A fully stocked first-aid kit and a fully charged fire extinguisher are vitally important safety accessories for any woodshop.

Table-Saw Tune-Up and Maintenance

A table saw does not come finely tuned and ready to do its best cutting straight from the box. Even if it was assembled by the dealer, it's likely to need fine adjustment and diagnosis. In this chapter, I'll explain how to set up your saw for accurate, safe, dependable use and how to keep it that way. The adjustments that I'll describe generally apply to all table-saw models; any differences between types of saws will be pointed out. To refresh your memory regarding the internal parts of a saw, you may want to refer to the saw anatomy illustration on p. 7. You should also find drawings of your particular saw in your owner's manual.

Initial and Periodic Tune-Ups

Many table-saw adjustments may need to be performed only once or twice during the lifetime of the saw. Others should be viewed as part of a regular periodic checkup. Some adjustments need to be performed more frequently, depending on the quality of your saw, how it's used, and whether it's moved around a lot. A more expensive, well-made saw will generally hold its adjustments longer than a lightweight, inexpensive saw.

A proper tune-up requires a particular sequence of adjustments, as listed in the sidebar on the facing page. It's important to perform them in the proper order because one step often affects the next. The procedures I discuss here include a thorough inspection of a saw, whether brand new or used. On a new saw, you're not likely to encounter serious problems such as loose bearings, but don't skip their inspection in any case.

A Tune-Up Checklist

WHETHER YOU JUST BOUGHT A NEW OR USED SAW or whether you simply want to get the most from your current saw, a thorough inspection and tune-up can work wonders. Here is a list of the steps to take. All of these procedures are addressed in this chapter. Make sure you perform the steps in the order listed.

- Inspect the arbor and bearings
- Clean and lubricate the internal mechanisms
- Eliminate gear backlash
- Inspect the pulley alignment and belts
- Set the blade-angle stops
- Stabilize the base
- Level and align the tables and throat plate
- Align the blade and miter-gauge slots
- Align the splitter
- Adjust the rip fence and miter gauge
- Clean and wax the work surfaces

Getting an Owner's Manual

If you don't have an owner's manual for your saw, you can request one from the manufacturer (see Sources on p. 197). You can find information on many manufacturers on the Internet. Some web sites provide parts lists and drawings, as well as information for ordering online.

Arbor and Bearings

The first things to check on a saw are the arbor and bearings. Wear or looseness in either can be a serious problem, resulting in excessive runout, where the spinning sawblade wobbles and cuts a kerf wider than the blade teeth. It's unlikely that a new saw will have problems in these areas, but if it does you'll want to find out right away, as you may want to return the saw. If you come across an old saw for sale with a bad arbor or bearings, I suggest you think twice about buying it. Even if you can find the parts, replacing them may cost you more time and money than the saw is worth.

To check the arbor and bearings, first unplug the saw and remove the blade. Inspect the arbor and flange for dirt and for burrs and nicks that have raised the metal. Some imperfections can be removed carefully with a fine-cut file. However, deep grooves that cause a sloppy blade fit probably call for replacement of the arbor.

To check the bearings, remove the drive belt(s) and turn the arbor by hand while feeling for any stiffness or coarseness in the movement. Grasp the arbor and gently pull up and down to check for any slack in the bearings. Roughness, resistance, or slack generally indicates faulty bearings in a new saw or worn bearings in an old saw.

Every table saw suffers runout to some small degree, even if the arbor and bearings are in great shape. Unfortunately, there is no such thing as an arbor flange that is precisely 90 degrees to the arbor. Most modern manufacturers press the flange onto the arbor and then turn it, resulting in a flange with less than 0.001-in. runout, which is acceptable. Saws with an added or loose arbor flange often don't fare as well. Minimizing arbor

To measure flange runout, place a dial indicator against the flange and slowly rotate the arbor. A magnetic base holds the dial indicator solidly in place.

runout is important because any runout at the flange multiplies toward the perimeter of a sawblade, affecting the quality of cut.

To measure runout of the flange, hold a dial indicator against the flange and slowly rotate the arbor (see the photo above). Runout should be less than 0.001 in. More than that will cause enough vibration in even a good sawblade to cause rough cutting and splintering. The best way to correct the problem is to remove the arbor assembly and take it to a machine shop for truing.

You should also check your blades for runout. In this context, runout refers to any deviation from true flatness, and there's no such thing as a perfectly flat blade. It's important to understand that operable runout, which is what affects your cutting, is the result of both blade runout and arbor runout combined. For example, take a 10-in.-dia. blade that is out of flat by 0.006 in. If you mount it on an arbor flange that has 0.001-in. runout, that 0.001 in. is multiplied by the 5-in. blade radius to create 0.005-in. runout at the perimeter of the blade. Add that 0.005-in. runout to the 0.006-in. runout in the blade itself, and you end up with a blade wobbling 0.011 in. at its perimeter—not good. I consider runout more than 0.006 in. to be excessive.

To check the operable runout of a blade, place a dial indicator at the perimeter of the blade body as you slowly rotate the blade. If runout varies all around, the cause is probably a warped blade. If the extremes are 180 degrees apart, the cause is more likely to be runout in the arbor flange.

Cleaning and Lubricating the Internal Parts

Regular cleaning and lubrication of a saw's internal parts are essential for smooth, accurate operation. I've never gotten organized enough to set a schedule for this; I just tend to it a few times a year, depending on how often I use the saw and whether I notice stiffness and resistance in the adjusting mechanisms. If you've never tended to the guts of your saw, now is a good time to do it.

CLEANING

Begin by vacuuming the interior and brushing off the gears. Pay particular attention to sawdust packed around the motor and the blade-height and blade-angle adjusting mechanisms. Take the opportunity to check the assemblies for excessive wear or damage, especially the teeth on the sector gears. (If these are worn excessively or if teeth are missing, the gears can be replaced.) Scrub the trunnion grooves and gear teeth using a rag or toothbrush and nonflammable solvent to clean off any pitch, grease, or crud from the parts. On new saws, the gears typically come with a thick packing of grease, which needs to be removed. Otherwise, the grease will accumulate sawdust, becoming a sticky mess gunking up the works.

LUBRICATING

Lubricate the gears and trunnion grooves. The best lubricants to use for these moving parts are ones that do not pick up a lot of sawdust, such as furniture wax or a dry lubricant. There are a number of dry lubricants on the market; ask at a bike shop. If you use wax, you can apply it with a brush (see the photo at right). There's no need to buff it off. To lubricate the entire length of the trunnion grooves, begin with the motor set at 90 degrees, clean the exposed sections, then crank the motor over to 45 degrees to access the remainder of the grooves.

The only other interior parts that may need lubrication are the sections of the two adjusting rods where they enter the cabinet and where their stop collars ride against the rack assemblies. In both places, you can loosen the stop collars and slide them back on the rods, then clean, wax, and return them to their original positions. Use lithium spray to lubricate assembly pivot points and other hard-to-access areas.

Most newer saws and motors are built with permanently sealed bearings, but if yours has lubrication fittings on the motor or arbor assemblies, squirt them with some light machine oil at least twice a year. Don't overdo it, and don't oil anything that doesn't sport an oil fitting. Exposed oil will only collect sawdust and congeal into a gummy substance. Rubber drive belts will also deteriorate if exposed to oil.

Apply wax to the sector gear teeth using a toothbrush. There's no need to buff it off.

Eliminating Gear Backlash

If you can turn the blade-tilting or height-adjustment wheel more than one-eighth of a turn without moving the blade, it means there is excessive play between the internal worm gear and its sector gear. This is called backlash, which can result in the blade shifting or dropping a bit during a cut. (Tightening the locking knob in the center of the tilt wheel only locks the position of the tilt; it does nothing to take out the play.) Backlash must be removed before you can accurately align the trunnion/carriage assembly to the miter slots.

With the saw unplugged, check for backlash by trying to move the arbor and carriage assembly by hand. First, tilt the carriage off the 90-degree stop, then grab the motor and try to shift it back and forth. There should not be any play in either direction. If there is, most saws can be adjusted, as explained next. (If you have problems with your particular saw, you can consult your owner's manual or call the manufacturer for technical support. But often, the adjustment will become apparent after scrutinizing the mechanisms.)

On a contractor's saw, remove the motor, turn the saw upside down, and loosen the screws that hold the wheel-bearing retainer to the outside of the saw body. You will then be able to shift the wheel downward. This forces the worm gear against the bevel-sector gear, producing a tighter fit. Retighten the screws and check that the wheel turns smoothly without binding, which can cause excessive wear on the meshing teeth.

On most cabinet saws, an adjustment bolt inside the cabinet at the front of the saw moves the worm gear against the sector gear for a tighter fit. Refer to your saw manual for specific instructions on the adjustment.

Unfortunately, not all saws provide an adjustment for stabilizing the carriage assembly. On certain saws, some backlash may exist even after making adjustments. On these saws, temporarily clamping the rear trunnion to its bracket will eliminate any play. Some older saws have a built-in trunnion lock to temporarily secure the carriage at any setting.

Pulley Alignment and Belt Inspection

To minimize vibration and noise on your saw, it's important that the pulleys on the arbor and motor shafts are aligned to each other and that the belt(s) are in good shape.

PULLEYS
To check the pulley alignment on a home-shop saw, lay a straightedge across the faces of the pulleys. The straightedge should contact both edges of each pulley (see the illustration on the facing page). If it doesn't, loosen the setscrew in the motor-shaft pulley, adjust the pulley as necessary, then tighten the setscrew.

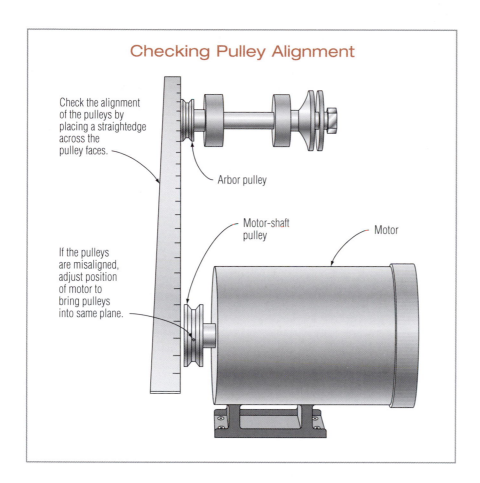

Checking Pulley Alignment

Check the alignment of the pulleys by placing a straightedge across the pulley faces.

Arbor pulley

Motor-shaft pulley

Motor

If the pulleys are misaligned, adjust position of motor to bring pulleys into same plane.

When you make this adjustment, it's best that the pulley is as close as possible to the motor bearing to prevent unnecessary strain on the shaft and bearings. If necessary, loosen the motor mount and slide the motor over into a better position. While you're at it, inspect the motor mount for damage or evidence of sliding. Lock washers on the motor-mount bolts should prevent the latter.

The stock pulleys on a contractor's saw are typically made of light-weight, die-cast aluminum. These can be out-of-round, contributing to saw vibration. Turned machine pulleys—available for most saws—are a much better option. You may need a small bearing puller to remove the pulley from the arbor, especially on an older saw. But it's easy to exchange the motor pulley, and this alone can help reduce vibration.

BELTS

The condition of a saw's belt or belts can also affect power and vibration. Most modern table saws employ V-belts, which ride against the inside walls of the pulleys. To maximize torque transmission, the sides of the belt need to make maximum contact with the pulley's inside walls. The shape of the belt should perfectly match the slope of the pulley walls and fill the pulley groove entirely.

The grooved belt on this Ridgid® saw is more pliable than a typical V-belt and transmits power better.

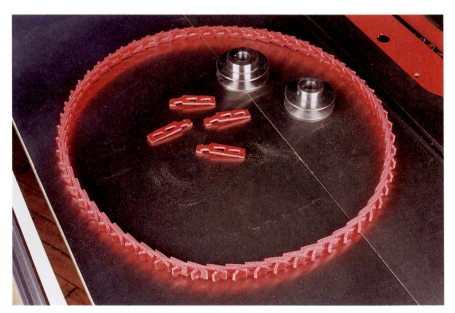

Segmented belts provide better pulley traction than standard V-belts because the links prevent the belt from taking on a set shape and slapping on the pulleys. The turned steel pulleys also shown here are more concentric than typical cast pulleys and reduce saw vibration.

A belt that is too wide will ride above the pulley rim, causing some loss of power. On the other hand, a belt that is narrow or worn will bottom out in the pulley's landing, reducing contact with the sides and causing slippage. The ensuing friction and heat can cause excessive wear to both the pulley and the belt. Worn or frayed belts will cause vibration and should be replaced. Vibration transmitted to the blade accounts for rough cutting even with the best of blades.

V-belts have a rubber body with interior cording that is strong enough to carry the load and resist stretching. Always replace worn belts with new ones that match the original. Never try to fit a new belt to a badly worn pulley; instead, replace the pulley. If your saw uses multiple belts, replace them all as a set, even if only one is worn. Otherwise, the load will be unevenly distributed, causing vibration and premature wear.

A V-belt is not really the best choice for a drive belt, especially on a contractor's saw, which typically uses a long belt. Often, this type of belt retains some memory of its packaged, oval shape and tends to "slap" in use, causing vibration. Some new-model saws employ a wide, flat, grooved belt that is more pliable and an excellent power transmitter (see the top photo on the facing page). A good replacement option for a contractor's saw is a segmented belt, which is made up of individual links (see the bottom photo on the facing page). This type of belt can't assume a set shape, thereby reducing vibration.

Setting the Blade-Angle Stops

Now that things are cleaned up inside your saw, check the accuracy of the blade-tilt stops. One stop should register the blade at 90 degrees to the tabletop, and the other stop should register it at 45 degrees. Begin with the 90-degree setting.

THE 90-DEGREE STOP

Raise the blade to nearly its full height, making sure that the tilt wheel is cranked fully over against the 90-degree stop without applying excessive pressure on the stop. Also make sure there is no sawdust or crud on the stop or on its area of contact on the bevel-sector gear. Place a large, accurate square on the table and against the body of the blade between the teeth. If the angle appears to need adjustment, crank the sector gear away from the stop and loosen the lock nut on the stop bolt. Turn the stop bolt in the direction necessary to correct the tilt (see the photo on p. 94). Crank the blade back over against the stop and recheck the setting with your square. Repeat the process until the blade stops at 90 degrees.

A more practical test, which will compensate for any errors in your square or eyesight is to check the accuracy of the cut itself. First, make sure that the locking knobs on the height and angle wheels are tightened. Then mill a piece of wood about 2 in. wide by about 18 in. long. Its thickness isn't important, but the piece must be planed flat and square, with its opposite edges parallel to each other. Mark a large X on the face of the board, as shown in the top illustration on p. 95. Set your miter gauge at 90 degrees, stand the board on edge, and crosscut through the center of

Save used belts to use as spares for temporary emergency use.

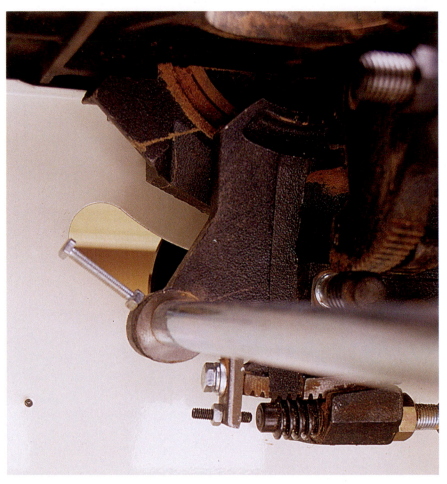

An Allen screw at the end of the sector gear provides an adjustable stop for setting the sawblade at 90 degrees.

the X. Flip one of the halves in relation to the other, then place both pieces against a good straightedge.

Any deviation from square will be doubled, making it easy to see. If necessary, adjust the tilt stop as described above and make another test cut. When the two pieces meet squarely end to end, you're set. Tighten the lock nut on the stop bolt while maintaining the stop bolt's position, then check the cut accuracy one last time. When you're satisfied, set the pointer on the tilt wheel to its 90-degree mark.

THE 45-DEGREE STOP

If your saw has a 45-degree stop, tilt the blade over until it stops. To check the angle, crosscut another accurately milled piece of scrap at 45 degrees, then place the two pieces against a try square as shown in the bottom illustration on the facing page. If the 45-degree setting is accurate, the pieces will form a 90-degree angle. If they don't, adjust the stop in the same manner as before.

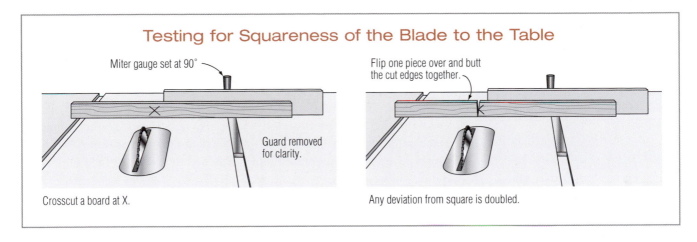

Testing for Squareness of the Blade to the Table

Miter gauge set at 90°

Guard removed for clarity.

Crosscut a board at X.

Flip one piece over and butt the cut edges together.

Guard removed for clarity.

Any deviation from square is doubled.

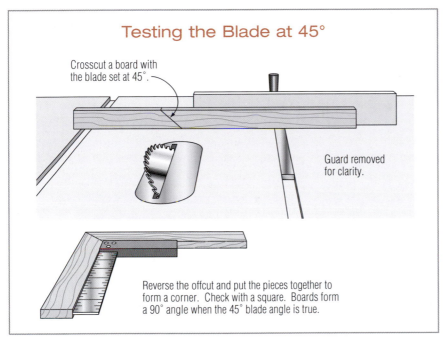

Testing the Blade at 45°

Crosscut a board with the blade set at 45°.

Guard removed for clarity.

Reverse the offcut and put the pieces together to form a corner. Check with a square. Boards form a 90° angle when the 45° blade angle is true.

Be aware that the stops will only get you close to the angle that you want. A little pressure more or less against the stop can make a difference. Turning the crank a little too much will almost always twist the carriage assembly. Whenever I need an accurate angle, I adjust the blade using a square or bevel gauge, then make test cuts to verify.

Stabilizing the Base

A table-saw base needs to sit solidly on the floor without rocking. Instability can be a safety hazard when cutting and can contribute to vibration. It's also best if the tabletop is level. To stabilize a saw that sits on a bolted-together stand, place a level on the tabletop, then loosen the bolts and shift the parts of the stand until the saw sits solidly on all of its legs with the top level. Retighten the bolts. For a saw with an enclosed base, strategically place shims under the base to level and steady it. Some saws include adjustable levelers for this purpose.

If your saw is lightweight or top-heavy, adding sandbags or bolting it to the floor will improve stability and reduce vibration. If you bolt your saw to a wood floor, check that the floor area underneath doesn't vibrate. You can also run the bolts through rubber pads under the saw feet to further reduce vibration. Outfeed tables attached to a saw can help improve stability as well.

Mark the Location

If you have to move your saw often, first mark its original stable position on the floor so that you can return it there later. Attaching a thin pad of wood or plastic to each foot helps prevent scratching your floor when moving the saw.

Aligning the Tables

Because the table surface is the reference used to present the workpiece to the blade, it needs to be as flat as possible to ensure accurate cuts. As discussed in chapter 2, an out-of-flat tabletop can affect cutting, particularly a dip or hump near the blade. However, not every deviation in a top's flatness will affect the accuracy of your cuts. The only way to really tell is to make cuts with variously sized pieces of wood, then check them for square.

A tabletop can also be twisted, where two diagonally opposed corners are higher than the others. Fortunately, a twisted top—unlike a humped or dipped top—can often be corrected, as explained on the facing page. It's important that any attached extensions be aligned to the main table as well. Table alignment should be taken care of before making the remaining adjustments discussed in this chapter.

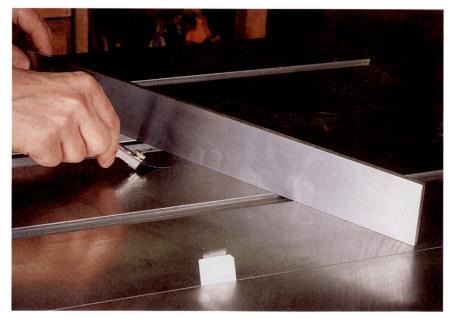

An accurate straightedge placed diagonally across the main table will reveal twist. The low spot between the table's two high corners can be measured with a feeler gauge.

THE MAIN TABLE

Begin by checking the flatness of the main table. I have been surprised to find that many tables are twisted; cast-iron tops are more flexible than you might think—especially many of today's lighter-weight tops. Aluminum tops are even more flexible.

To check the main table for twist, place an accurate straightedge across the table diagonally in both directions. A twisted top will expose a low spot between one pair of corners and a high spot between the opposite pair (see the photo on the facing page). Sometimes a top may be twisted simply because the top of the body or cabinet isn't flat. In that case, you can shim under the bolts until the top is flat.

Sometimes a twist is caused by the weight of a long extension table and rails and maybe an overarm blade guard cantilevered off the side of the saw. Even if an extension table has legs, the legs may be standing on an uneven floor, effectively pulling down the side of the saw table. In either case, proper shimming may bring the tabletop back into flat.

EXTENSION WINGS

The extension wings need to be adjusted flush with and in the same plane as the main table. I check the joint first with a short straightedge, then I check the span of the main table and extension table with a long straightedge (see the photo below).

In order for the table and extension to meet in the same plane, the edges of both must be 90 degrees to the top. I've found that this is rare and that it's often necessary to shim the joint to make the two surfaces level.

Precision Straightedge

A precision-machined 3-ft. or 4-ft. straightedge is an invaluable tool for both woodworking- and machine-tool maintenance. I couldn't do without mine. But they're not cheap: Expect to pay $70 to $160.

Use a long straightedge and shims to set the extension wings level and flush to the main table.

It's also best to first check both mating surfaces for any foreign matter or imperfections. Clean the edges and smooth out any protrusions using a fine, flat file.

To shim the joint, you must first loosen the bolts enough to insert shims either at the top or the bottom of the joint to drive the wing up or down as necessary. Gauging the number and thickness of the shims is a trial-and-error affair. For shims, you can use anything that you can find around the shop, including paper, cellophane, or aluminum from a soda can. Use a clamp at each end of the joint to hold it flush as you tighten up the bolts. Sometimes it takes a bit of tapping with a dead-blow hammer to align.

Pressed-steel wings are often twisted but can be made relatively flat by loosening their connections to the fence rails, adjusting the position of each connection, then retightening the bolts.

EXTENSION TABLES

Extension tables to the side and rear of the saw are great for supporting workpieces during and after cutting. Side tables are typically bolted to the main table and set flush and level to it. It's best if a bolted-on table is supported on its own legs to prevent its weight from introducing wind into the main tabletop. A rear outfeed table can be freestanding or attached, and it doesn't hurt to have it set just a bit lower than the main table (but never higher). You can use a long, jointed board for checking the alignment of an extension table with the main table.

THE THROAT PLATE

The throat plate is an important part of the table surface and needs to be stable and flush to the table. Stock aluminum throat plates typically have leveling screws and a wide opening that allows the blade to be tilted for bevel cutting. However, narrow pieces of wood can wedge in the opening, causing them to be thrown back at the operator.

I suggest that you replace the stock throat plate with a zero-clearance throat plate that leaves no open space to either side of the raised blade. You won't be able to use it for bevel cutting, but it will serve you much better for the majority of your cutting, which is at 90 degrees anyway. A zero-clearance throat plate provides solid bearing right up to the blade, resulting in safer cuts that will also be cleaner because fully supported wood fibers are less likely to fray or tear out. Throat plates are easy to make (see the sidebar on the facing page). Commercial throat-plate blanks are also available for most table saws (see the photo on p. 100).

For throat plates with leveling screws, use a short straightedge as a guide to level the throat plate to the tabletop. Adjust the leveling screws or shim the underside of the plate with tape to bring it flush to the tabletop. Make sure that the plate doesn't rock in any direction. Some woodworkers set the plate a hair low in front to prevent a workpiece from

Custom Throat Plates

THE STOCK THROAT PLATES THAT COME WITH A TABLE SAW have too wide of an opening for safe, clean cutting. I prefer to make my own zero-clearance throat plates that support the workpiece right to the sides of the blades.

You can make the throat plates out of almost any dry, stable hardwood at hand, avoiding figured or defective stock, which might compromise stability. When making test cuts, first thickness-plane the stock to be exactly flush with the tabletop. Once you get the exact thickness setting, plane enough stock to make several plates because it's handy to have a number of throat plates with different-sized openings.

If you don't have a planer, or if you want to make your plates adjustable, you can use ½-in.-thick hardwood plywood or ultra-high molecular weight (UHMW) plastic, which is very slick and stable. To make these plates adjustable, install setscrews that will rest on the tabs in the throat-plate opening.

When sizing the plate, take measurements from the throat opening rather than from the stock plate, which tends to be undersized. I use the stock plate only to lay out the profile for the rounded ends. Cut close to the layout line, then use a disk sander for final fitting. Sand a bit at a time until the fit is snug. You may need to chamfer the bottom edge of the throat plate slightly to get it to seat properly in its opening. If you are replacing a particularly thin plate, you may need to rabbet the underside of a ½-in.-thick plate to fit it into its opening. Alternatively, you could glue a heavier piece to the underside of thin stock. Drill a finger hole at the front of any throat plate for easy removal, and ease the edges of the hole for comfort.

To cut the saw kerf in the throat plate, clamp the blank down using a narrow board spanning the table-

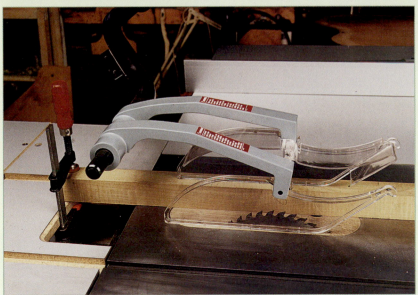

To cut the blade slot in a zero-clearance throat plate, clamp the blank to the table using a long, narrow board that spans the tabletop. Raise the spinning blade slowly into the throat plate.

saw top (see the photo above). Then turn on the saw and raise the blade slowly into the plate. On many saws, the standard blade will not retract enough to allow you to completely insert the throat-plate blank. In this case, use a smaller-diameter blade to start the kerf, then switch to the desired blade to finish the cut. If you don't have a smaller blade, you can chisel a narrow starter channel to accommodate the top edge of the blade.

After cutting the kerf, mark out the splitter slot, aligning it with the kerf. Then cut the slot using a bandsaw or a small handsaw. Waxing the plate afterward will minimize wood movement and reduce feed friction. To prevent any possibility of the plate lifting in use, you can attach a small wood catch or metal washer to the underside at the rear. You can also fit the throat plate with a shopmade splitter (see the sidebar on p. 68).

catching on it. This is a safe practice, but I prefer to keep the plate as level as possible because the accuracy of some joinery operations depends on a perfectly level plate.

Shopmade or commercial throat inserts provide zero clearance around the blade, making for safer, cleaner cutting.

Aligning the Miter-Gauge Slots to the Blade

For accurate ripping and crosscutting, the sawblade should be perfectly parallel to the miter-gauge slots. Unfortunately, a machine seldom comes exactly aligned from the factory. For ripping, you can compensate for this misalignment by adjusting the rip fence parallel to the sawblade. However, that won't correct the problem for crosscutting because a miter gauge, crosscut sled, or similar jig must travel in the miter slots. And if the slots aren't parallel to the blade, the blade will cut into the work with both the front and then the back of the blade. Changing the angle of approach won't correct the problem.

To determine if the blade is misaligned to the miter slots, you'll need to measure from the blade to a miter slot. There are a number of great commercial products made specifically for this purpose (as well as other machine tuning), but I find that an inexpensive dial indicator clamped to a miter gauge does well for this job (see the sidebar on the facing page). A dial indicator provides measurements in thousandths of an inch for great accuracy and is easy to read while you're adjusting the alignment.

If you don't want to buy a dial indicator, I'll also discuss a low-tech method for aligning your blade to its miter slots. Both methods that I'll explain require the use of a miter gauge that fits snugly in its slots. Yours may not, so I'll cover that first.

Dial Indicators

I HIGHLY RECOMMEND GETTING A DIAL INDICATOR FOR YOUR SHOP because it's a very useful tool for setting up and aligning machines. It can take measurements in thousandths of an inch, displaying them clearly on the dial face, and it will help you accurately measure runout on arbors, flanges, chucks, bits, and blades. You can also use it to align machine fences and jointer and planer knives, among other things.

To get the most from a dial indicator, you'll want a magnetic base for attaching it to machine tables, fences, and other surfaces. The base should include a post and an adjustable arm for positioning the dial indicator as needed (see the photo on p. 88). You can buy a decent-quality dial indicator and magnetic base for as little as $35 (see Sources on p. 197).

To effectively widen a miter-gauge bar that fits sloppily in its grooves, pound a series of chisel grooves across the edge of the bar.

TUNING THE MITER-GAUGE FIT

The bar on a stock miter gauge often fits sloppily in its slots. One way to eliminate this side-to-side play is by slotting the edges of the bar with a cold chisel (see the photo above). The raised metal around the chiseled depressions essentially widen the soft metal bar, taking out the slop. Space the depressions evenly all along one or both edges of the bar—not just in a section or two. You want the bar to stay snug even when it's extended partially off the table. If you've made it too snug, run a fine-cut file lightly over the chiseled edge of the bar.

Although this fix will last quite a while, it's only temporary; eventually the soft metal will wear down, producing slop again. If you use a miter gauge a lot (I don't, as explained later), consider buying a better-fitting

Some miter-gauge bars include Allen screws or other fittings for adjusting the width of the bar to better fit its slot.

A dial indicator provides an immediate readout for adjusting the blade parallel to the miter groove. A bar clamp locked onto the rear trunnions provides a lever for easy adjustment of the trunnion position.

aftermarket bar. Some have built-in adjustments (see the top photo). Some are longer than stock bars, which helps create a better fit because any deviations are spread over a greater distance.

Aligning the Blade to the Miter-Gauge Slots

Contractor's saw

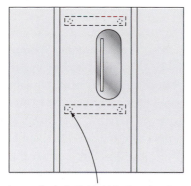

Loosen the bolts that hold the trunnions to the tabletop. Shift the trunnions relative to the table to align the blade and miter slots.

Cabinet saw

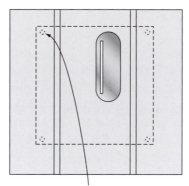

Loosen the bolts that secure the tabletop to the saw base. Shift the top to align the blade and miter slots.

MAKING THE ADJUSTMENTS USING A DIAL INDICATOR

Now that your miter-gauge bar fits well, you're ready to make the blade-to-miter-slot adjustment. With the power disconnected, elevate the blade just short of its maximum height. Never crank the blade hard against its stops, which will twist the internal mechanisms.

Screw the dial indicator to a piece of wood that extends out toward the blade. It doesn't matter if the miter gauge isn't at a perfect 90-degree angle to the blade. Clamp the wood so that the plunger is lightly depressed against the perimeter of the blade plate, not against a tooth (see the bottom photo on the facing page).

Rotate the scale on the dial indicator until its reference pointer is at zero. Using a felt-tipped pen, make a reference mark on the blade near the plunger. Slide the miter gauge to the opposite end of the blade, then rotate the blade until your reference mark is under the plunger. The dial indicator will show the amount of difference between the two positions, indicating the amount of misalignment between the plane of the blade and the miter slot.

The reason for rotating the blade is that no blade is perfectly flat. Therefore, you can't just measure the distance at the front and rear of a blade without introducing error. For the same reason, you shouldn't measure to a straightedge placed against the blade.

To bring the blade and miter slots in line with each other, you'll need to adjust either the carriage or the tabletop, depending on the type of saw (see the illustration above). On portable saws and home-shop saws, adjust the carriage. Slightly loosen the bolts that hold the trunnions to the top. Don't loosen them too much; it's best to have just a bit of resistance when you're trying to move the carriage only a few thousandths of an inch. You can tap the trunnion with a mallet to move it, but I find it much easier to clamp the trunnion and carriage assembly together with an F-style bar clamp, then use the bar as a lever to move the rear of the carriage (see the bottom photo on p. 102).

After you make an adjustment, you may need to reset the reference pointer on the dial indicator before rechecking the alignment. When the dial indicator registers the same distance at the front and rear of the blade, tighten the trunnion bolts, then recheck the alignment. It may take several efforts to get the alignment dead on, but it's worth it, and you may only have to do this once or twice for the life of the saw.

On a stationary cabinet saw, the trunnion mechanisms are fixed to the cabinet, so it's the tabletop that you need to move instead. Loosen the tabletop bolts a bit, then tap the edge of the tabletop to bring it into proper relation to the blade.

THE LOW-TECH APPROACH

If you don't have a dial indicator, you can use a long piece of wood and a feeler gauge instead. Spring-clamp the piece of wood to the miter gauge as before, but this time bring the wood right up to the side of the teeth. Using the piece of wood as a reference, first determine whether the front or rear of the blade is closest to the miter slot. Mark a tooth at that spot with chalk or a felt marker.

Next, rotate the marked tooth to the opposite end of the throat-plate slot and take a feeler-gauge measurement of the gap there (see the photo

Enlarging Bolt Holes

Sometimes trunnion bolt holes are too small to allow sufficient movement for proper adjustment. In that case, simply drill or file the holes to elongate them in the proper direction.

If you don't have a dial indicator, you can use a feeler gauge to measure the distance between the blade and a piece of wood clamped to a miter gauge.

on the facing page). As mentioned in the previous section, don't trust measurements unless they're taken from the same spot on a rotated blade. If the difference between the front and rear of the blade is more than 0.003 in., adjust the alignment as explained above.

Aligning the Splitter to the Blade

For optimum performance and safety, the splitter or riving knife must be properly aligned with the sawblade. If misaligned, it can steer a workpiece into or away from the rip fence, leading to inaccurate cuts or difficult feeding. Stock splitters are typically thinner than the blade, whereas aftermarket splitters vary from about $\frac{3}{32}$ in. thick to $\frac{1}{8}$ in. thick. A stock splitter typically aligns with the center of the blade, but I prefer to shim it out so it's even with the right side of the teeth (the side closest to the fence). This way, it will firmly hold the workpiece against the fence, resulting in a clean—as well as safe—cut.

To adjust a splitter, loosen the bolts that attach it to the carriage assembly. With the blade set at 90 degrees, use a square to set the splitter perpendicular to the table. Using a straightedge, line it up with the right side of the blade. The flimsy stock splitters that come with most saws bend out of shape easily, but they can just as easily be bent back into shape.

Adjusting the Rip Fence

For proper cutting, a rip fence must be adjusted parallel to the blade. The faces must also be straight and flat, as well as square to the table. A rip fence that is out of alignment with the blade will cause a number of problems. A fence that angles away from the rear of the blade will cause the workpiece to skew away from the fence, burning the waste side of the cut and creating a hollow workpiece edge in the process.

The more dangerous situation is when the fence angles toward the rear of the blade. In that case, the workpiece will bind between the fence and the teeth at the rear of the blade, burning the workpiece and inviting kickback if no splitter or riving knife is installed. Don't bother to adjust the rip fence until the blade has been adjusted parallel to the miter-gauge slots, as discussed previously.

To check your fence alignment, lock the fence in position and measure from it to the opposite ends of the miter-gauge slots, again using the dial indicator attached to the miter gauge. Alternatively, you can place blocks of ¾-in.-thick stock into the miter-gauge slot at each end, then gently lock the rip fence against the blocks to see if they contact the fence at the same time. If not, the alignment needs adjustment.

Many old-style stock fences made of stamped steel are adjusted by loosening the two bolts on the top of the fence, moving the body until it is parallel to the miter-gauge slot, then retightening the screws. An adjustment screw at the front of the fence regulates the grip of the hook on the back rail that locks the rear of the fence in place.

Biesemeyer-style fences are adjusted by turning Allen screws on the crossbar that rides on the fence rail. The fence needs to be removed to adjust the screws, then replaced to test the alignment (see the photo at left below). This trial-and-error adjustment isn't difficult, though, and doesn't take long.

I like to set my rip fence so that it is no more than 0.001 in. farther from the rear of the blade than it is at the front of the blade. This way, the rear teeth just barely touch the workpiece, providing a smooth, unburned cut without steering the workpiece away from the fence. I use a feeler gauge or dial indicator to measure the distance between the fence and the teeth.

The faces of a fence should also be square to the table all along their lengths. Check them with a good square. A tilted fence can result in inaccurate cuts when ripping stock of different thicknesses, edge-grooving, or tenoning when using the fence as a reference surface. A few fences provide for making this adjustment (see the photo at right below). If yours doesn't, you can add an auxiliary fence and shim it out as necessary.

Make Sure the Fence is Straight

Old-style stamped-steel fences are notorious for not having straight faces. Whatever fence you have, check its straightness using an accurate straightedge. If the fence is bowed or twisted, add an auxiliary wood fence, shimming it to correct any imperfections.

To adjust a Biesemeyer-style fence parallel to the blade, remove the fence from its rail and adjust the Allen screws on the crossbar that presses against the rail.

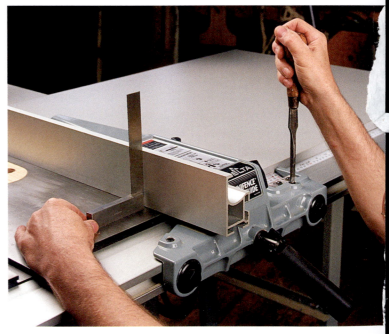

Some fences, like this Unifence, provide adjustments for setting the face of the fence perpendicular to the saw table.

Once you've set the miter gauge at 90 degrees to the blade, adjust the setscrew that presses against the stop.

Adjusting the Miter Gauge

An accurate stock miter gauge is a contradiction in terms. Most of them are sloppily made, and I almost never use mine. But a lot of woodworkers do use them, so I'll address here how to adjust miter-gauge stops.

Begin by placing a large square against the gauge and the blade body, avoiding the teeth. When the relationship appears square, lock the miter-gauge head on its body. Next, crosscut a 3-in. piece off of a ¾-in. by 1½-in. by 18-in. board. Flip one of the cut pieces and place the sawn edges together against a straightedge.

Just as when you made a test cut earlier to check the blade perpendicularity to the table, any deviation from 90 degrees will be doubled when you put the sawn edges together (see the top illustration on p. 95). Readjust the miter-gauge angle and make more test cuts as necessary until the two sawn edges meet perfectly. Then set the stop and indicator so you'll be able to quickly set the gauge to 90 degrees repeatedly (see the photo above).

To set the miter-gauge stop at 45 degrees, adjust the gauge to approximately 45 degrees using a drafting triangle or sliding bevel gauge. Then crosscut a piece of scrap wood as explained above. Flip one of the pieces, then put the pieces together to form a corner as when making test cuts for checking the bevel angle of a blade (see the bottom illustration on p. 95). Check the corner using a square. Once again, any deviation from 90 degrees will be doubled. Readjust the miter-gauge angle as necessary until an exact 45-degree angle is achieved. Finally, set the 45-degree miter-gauge stop.

Cleaning and Maintaining Work Surfaces

A clean, smooth, waxed saw table is essential for safe, accurate, easy feeding of workpieces, as well as for the longevity of your saw. Wax reduces feed friction and helps prevent rust. I clean and wax my saw table and accessories whenever I start encountering feed resistance, which usually works out to three or four times a year.

Begin by cleaning the table. On a new saw, you may first need to wipe off the heavy antirust protectant using lots of mineral spirits and rags. On an old saw, you can remove heavier rust and stains using 400-grit wet/dry sandpaper lubricated with mineral spirits. Metal polish and coarse automobile rubbing compound also do a good job of rust and stain removal. Most tables can simply be scrubbed with mineral spirits and coarse steel wool to remove any light rust, pitch, gum deposits, and old wax.

Next, apply a thin coat of wax, rubbing it into the entire surface, including the miter-gauge slots. I use furniture paste wax, but most car and floor waxes will work equally well. Avoid floor waxes that contain antislip additives, and don't use products that contain silicone, which can cause finishing problems if it contaminates a work surface.

Allow the wax to dry to a haze, then buff it off. As long as all of the excess is removed, there's no danger of contaminating a work surface. Even if a small amount is transferred to the workpiece, normal sanding will remove it. I also clean and wax my saw's fence rails, extension tables, and rip fences and wipe down any plastic parts with a damp cloth.

Wax and other surface coatings help to protect the saw from rust but won't stop it. Rust is always ready to attack, so it's important to keep the table free of moisture. Common sense will tell you not to set drinks, green wood, or damp rags on the table. However, a more pernicious form of moisture is condensation—caused by a cold metal surface coming in contact with warm humid air from the outside or perhaps from a nearby clothes dryer. In these cases, a cardboard or specially designed cover can help protect the metal.

Preventing Rust

Rust is most common on tools that sit unused for long periods. If you're not going to be using your equipment for some months, it might be wise to lightly coat the top with oil or thin grease.

The Table-Saw Workstation

Properly set up and configured, the table saw is much more than just the primary tool in your woodworking arsenal. Along with its attendant fixtures, accessories, and extension tables, it's actually a workstation where you perform some of the most critical processes in woodworking. As such, it's important to carefully consider the saw's ideal placement in the shop as well as its lighting, wiring, dust collection, and relationship to other tools in your shop.

Saw Placement

The table saw is the heart of the shop in a number of ways. Not only is it central to many woodworking operations, but it's also often physically located in the middle of the shop and is the tool around which other processes often revolve. Unlike most other stationary woodshop tools, the table saw requires space on all four sides for ripping and crosscutting large workpieces.

For a table saw, a working space 17 ft. long and 12 ft. wide will accommodate most of the boards needed for many woodworking projects. The 8 ft. in front of the blade and the 8 ft. behind it allow enough infeed and outfeed room for ripping 8-ft.-long boards or panels. And if you situate the saw with 6½ ft. to the right of the blade and 5½ ft. to the left, you'll have plenty of room for crosscutting boards almost 8 ft. long.

If your shop doesn't allow you to dedicate such a large, permanent space to a table saw, think mobile. A good mobile base allows you to easily move a saw about in the shop to gain cutting room when needed (see the

Set up your table saw in a well-lit, convenient location, with saw accessories close at hand and as much space around the saw as you can afford.

A mobile base allows you to move your table saw around in a small shop to create infeed and outfeed areas as needed.

photo above). For that matter, you can leave your saw stationary and put surrounding machinery on mobile bases for clearing room around the saw when handling large workpieces.

You can also take advantage of open doors and windows by aiming long workpieces through them when ripping. For very small shops or garages, a portable saw can easily be moved about to make the most of the space that you do have. You can even take it outside if you're really cramped.

Arranging Machinery for Workflow

Table-saw placement

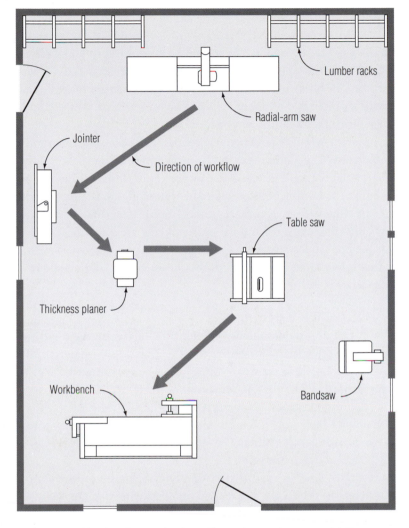

Arrange machines to suit your order of operations and economize movement. In the example shown here, work begins near the lumber racks, where boards are cut to rough length on the radial-arm saw. Workpieces are then milled at the jointer and planer before moving to the table saw for cutting to final size. Finally, joint-fitting and assembly takes place at the workbench.

Avoid Surprises

When possible, place your table saw so you're facing your shop entrance when working. This can prevent you from being startled from behind by visitors when concentrating on a cut.

Your table saw's placement in relation to other tools and operations is important because it affects workflow. Try to arrange your machines to follow your particular order of operations and to economize movement as much as possible. For example, my work generally begins at the cutoff saw near my lumber rack, where I crosscut boards to rough length. From there, I move to the nearby jointer and planer to do my initial stock dressing. After that, work moves to the table saw for cutting to final size (see the illustration on p. 111). For more information on machine placement and general shop setup, check out *The Workshop Book* by Scott Landis (The Taunton Press, 1991).

illustration on p. 111).

Wiring

Whatever type of saw you have, it should be connected to an appropriate electrical circuit—for reasons of both safety and efficiency. Most saws that are marketed for home use, including portable and contractor-style saws, come with motors rated at about 1½ hp. The horsepower, voltage, and amperage ratings for a motor can be found on its information plate.

The motors on these saws come wired for 115 volts, the common U.S. household current, making them ready to plug in and use without any need for special wiring. Because these motors draw around 15 amps, a saw should be plugged into a dedicated circuit that won't serve any other tools at the same time the saw is running. Since motors can draw more than their specified amperage upon startup, the circuit breaker should be rated at 20 amps. For Underwriters Laboratories (UL) approval, a 115-volt motor that draws more than 15 amps should use a special plug and matching receptacle.

230-VOLT CIRCUITS

A 230-volt circuit provides a more efficient use of electricity, resulting in fewer circuit overloads and longer motor life. The 1½-hp induction motors on most home-shop saws are dual-voltage motors, meaning they can be wired for either 115 or 230 volts. If you have a 230-volt circuit in your shop, it's definitely to your advantage to wire the saw motor for 230-volt use. If you don't have a 230-volt circuit, it's usually not difficult for an electrician to install one. Whenever adding or changing wiring, be sure local electrical codes are adhered to.

To rewire the motor for 230-volt use, remove the lid on the wiring box that's attached to the motor. Under the lid is a wiring diagram for changing the voltage. Once you've switched the wiring connections in the box, you'll need to replace the standard 115-volt plug on the end of the cord with a 230-volt plug (available at hardware stores).

ELECTRICAL OUTLETS AND CORDS

Ideally, the electrical outlet for the saw should be as close at hand as possible. For one thing, you don't want to have to use an extension cord (see the sidebar on the facing page). For another, it's important to be able to easily disconnect the power for saw maintenance and blade changing.

Since the table saw is often placed in the center of the shop, the power cord typically has to run across the floor to a wall outlet. If so, keep from tripping over an electrical cord by using a shopmade or commercial cord cover that's grooved on the underside to accommodate the cord (see

Needs of 3-hp to 5-hp Saws

If you're planning to buy a stationary saw with a motor ranging from 3 hp to 5 hp, you'll need a 230-volt circuit because these saws require it.

Extension Cords

ELECTRICAL EXTENSION CORDS INTRODUCE CURRENT RESISTANCE, which can cause a loss of amps to a motor. The longer the cord and the lighter weight it is, the greater the resistance. Running a motor with insufficient current can cause the motor to run hotter and slower than normal. It is best not to use an extension cord on a table saw. However, if you must, make sure the cord is as short as possible and at least as heavy as the saw's motor wire.

the photo at right). Cord housings are often available at office-supply stores.

Sometimes an outlet can be installed under the saw or extension table. Outlets set face up into the floor of a woodshop are definitely not a good idea because they'll just clog with dust. However, an outlet that sits above the floor on a short post works well and makes for easy power disconnects. Although overhead outlets work for some machines, they're often in the way at the table saw, especially when cutting sheet goods or large panels.

SWITCH PLACEMENT AND MODIFICATION

If your saw switch is mounted on the right side of the saw, consider moving it to the left if possible. Because most table-saw operations take place from the left side of the blade, it makes sense to place the switch there. When you are standing to the left of the blade and reaching over for a switch on the right side of the saw, you put your body in line with the blade, increasing the potential for injury. On most saws, moving the switch to the left side isn't difficult. It's usually just a matter of drilling a new mounting hole and rerouting the wire. Just make sure you have enough wire on the switch to reach the new location.

A shopmade knee switch is another feature that provides convenience as well as safety. My knee switch is simply a length of wood hinged to the fence rail with a cutout for finger access to the on switch (see the photo on p. 114). A block of wood glued to the back presses against the off button, effectively turning the entire piece of wood into a giant "panic switch" that can easily be hit in an instant. For example, I have been in a predicament where a workpiece kerf closed on the blade and I was afraid to let go of it to turn off the saw. In such situations, a large knee switch is an extra edge on safety. Even during ordinary operations, it's helpful not having to feel around for small buttons.

Lighting

Safe, accurate work at the table saw requires good overhead lighting that casts no shadows and creates no glare. Ideally, lots of natural light is the best choice, but that's often not an option. Instead, a fluorescent light fixture positioned above your saw with incandescent lighting to either side

A cord cover prevents tripping over cords snaking across the floor to the table saw.

An oversized knee switch allows you to turn the saw off quickly without taking your hands off the workpiece. Turning the saw on, however, requires deliberately reaching through the cutout to push the on button.

can give you plenty of light with no perceptible fluorescent flicker. You can test a lighting scheme by standing a 12-in. dowel on the table-saw surface and adjusting the lighting so the dowel casts no heavy shadows. General shop light can be improved by painting the walls and ceiling white to help reflect available light.

Dust Collection at the Table Saw

Making piles of sawdust is one of the table saw's many talents. Dust from every cut is discharged in several directions. The majority is packed into the blade gullets between the teeth, then ejected beneath the saw table. Above the table, a steady stream of dust is thrown toward the operator. Last, the smallest and most unhealthy dust particles remain in the air for us to breathe, finally settling as a film on all shop surfaces. Some sort of dust collection at the table saw is essential to health and general shop safety.

The problem is that most table saws sold in the United States aren't well suited to dust collection, either below or above the table. Contractor's saws are particularly problematic because of the wide open base. Some manufacturers offer an optional base plate with a dust port for connection to a dust collector (see the top photo on the facing page). However, a lot of dust still escapes from the open back of the saw.

Cabinet saws are better at capturing dust because of their enclosed bases, but they're still not very efficient because the cabinet is not sealed

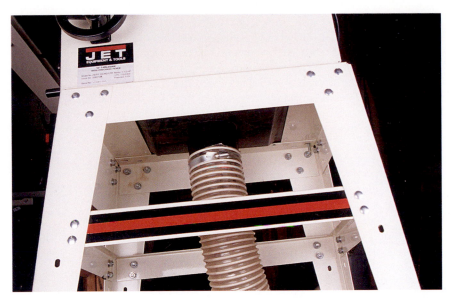

Outfitting a contractor's saw for dust collection requires installing a panel with a dust port under the saw cabinet. For better dust collection, the back of the saw should also be covered with a panel.

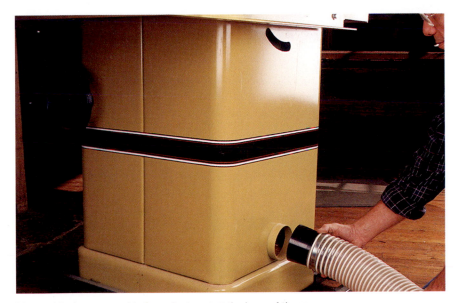

Most cabinet saws provide for a dust port at the base of the saw.

by any means. For dust-collection purposes, many cabinet saws offer only a port at the base of the cabinet that can be connected to a dust-collector hose (see the bottom photo above). Instead of a port, there may be a panel that can be replaced with an optional port attachment from the manufacturer. Newer-model cabinet saws feature an internal ramp to help direct the sawdust to the collector port.

To their credit, a few manufacturers are improving dust collection by taking cues from European table-saw design. Some newer-model portable

Doing the Best with Dust

Although sealing up a saw can help improve dust collection, don't expect miracles. The truth is that without a dust chute surrounding the blade, you're fighting poor dust-collection design.

Dust in the Wind

IN AN ENCLOSED SHOP, FINE DUST PARTICLES can float high in the air long after a cut is made. These fine particles are a real health hazard and should be evacuated or filtered. If you don't have good air circulation to the outside, an ambient air cleaner will quietly filter the finest dust particles from the air in your shop. A number of models and sizes are available to suit any size shop (see Sources on p. 197).

An ambient air cleaner filters from the shop air the very fine dust that is most harmful to the lungs.

and home-shop table saws include a dust chute that partially surrounds the blade (see the photo on p. 41). The chute, which is connected to a dust collector, efficiently gathers the dust right at the source. This system has been standard on European saws for some time.

For capturing dust above the table, a blade cover with a dust port does the trick. This type of cover is standard on European saws (see the bottom photo on p. 40). For saws sold in the United States, there are several after-market blade covers available (see "Better Blade Covers" on p. 70).

SEALING YOUR SAW

For saws without a dust chute, the best approach to improving dust collection is to seal up as much of the saw as possible. On cabinet saws, you can apply silicone to any small openings on the saw's body. For larger openings, such as the area between the tabletop and the cabinet, you can use duct tape. Taping the interior walls to the floor also helps. As for the large handwheel slot on the front of the saw, you can attach a slotted piece of inner tube to help seal the opening. Adding a shopmade inclined ramp of

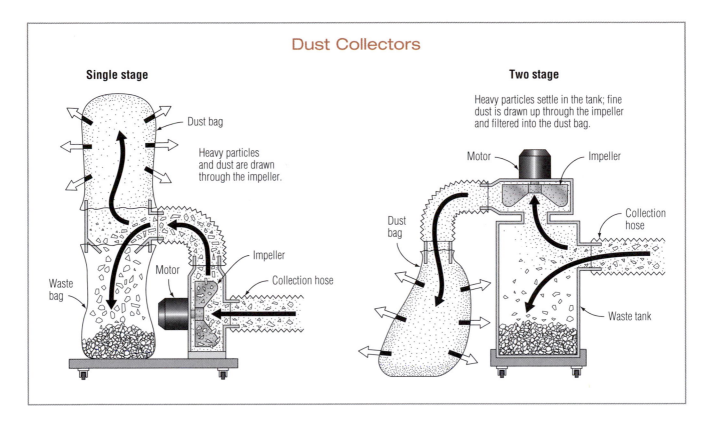

Dust Collectors

Single stage

Dust bag

Heavy particles and dust are drawn through the impeller.

Impeller

Collection hose

Motor

Waste bag

Two stage

Heavy particles settle in the tank; fine dust is drawn up through the impeller and filtered into the dust bag.

Motor

Impeller

Collection hose

Dust bag

Waste tank

sheet metal or plastic laminate to older saws can help direct dust toward a low-placed dust port.

Sealing up a contractor's saw is another challenge altogether. Because the motor hangs out the open back of the saw, it's difficult to seal up this saw, but that's what you have to do to capture the dust. Because most sawing is done with the blade set at 90 degrees, you can make a simple removable back to fit the saw set up for this angle. When a different angle is needed, you can remove the back easily.

DUST COLLECTORS

The first dust collector I tried using on my table saw was a shop vacuum, simply because I had one. Unfortunately, even industrial-quality shop vacs don't move enough air to be effective on most table saws. A table saw, like most shop machinery, requires a minimum of about 300 cubic feet per minute (cfm) of airflow at the point of connection for effective dust collection. An industrial shop vacuum typically produces only about 140 cfm. Most other shop vacuums produce only 100 cfm to 120 cfm and have a limited hose-diameter capacity.

The one exception is that a shop vac will work on a saw that incorporates a dust chute. As previously discussed, the dust chute partially surrounds the blade underneath the table and includes a port that can be connected to a shop vacuum or dust collector. The chute effectively retains the dust in an area small enough for a shop vac to evacuate.

For most table saws, though, I recommend a dust collector that is rated higher than 350 cfm. Any commercially available dust collector with at least a 1-hp motor should have enough drawing power for the table saw.

Dust collectors are available as either single-stage or two-stage units (see the illustration on p. 117). Single-stage systems draw all of the sawdust directly into the blower impellers. Heavy particles then drop below into a bag or other container, and fine dust is filtered by the upper bag. Two-stage systems draw particles into a tank or cyclone first, where the heavy particles drop, leaving only the fine dust to pass through the impeller blades and into the filter.

Both types of units have their pros and cons. Single-stage systems are generally less expensive and can be easier to empty out because the chips and sawdust end up in an easily detachable bag. However, single-stage systems are very noisy, and metal pieces that accidentally enter the system can damage the blades or cause sparks that can potentially ignite a dust fire. Two-stage systems are more expensive but tend to last longer because there is less wear on the impeller, housing, and motor.

Single-stage dust collectors There are two types of single-stage dust collectors: one is a small, single-bag unit, and the other is a double-bag unit that is often mounted on a mobile stand. A single-bag unit is powerful enough to use with a portable saw and lightweight enough to move around easily on a job site. Just be prepared to empty the small dust bag often.

A double-bag unit—typically 1 hp to 2 hp—is powerful and capacious enough to handle planer and jointer shavings as well as table-saw waste.

A conversion lid placed on a waste can between the saw and a single-stage dust collector creates a two-stage system because the heavy dust falls into the can before reaching the dust-collector impeller.

Fitted with a quick disconnect, it can easily be moved from machine to machine. These units are tall, though, and can be top-heavy. In some cases, this can make them awkward to use in a cramped shop. Note that you can convert a single-stage collector into a two-stage collector by employing a conversion lid that directs heavy waste into a trash can while allowing the finer dust to continue on to the dust collector (see the photo on the facing page).

Two-stage dust collectors There are also two types of double-stage collectors: a barrel-type unit and a cyclone unit. A barrel-type unit is fairly low profile. Because it's shorter than a table saw, it won't interfere with handling or feeding large workpieces. Cyclones are more efficient but are very tall and hardly portable.

Central dust collection Depending on the size of the woodshop, many woodworkers find it convenient to connect all of their machines to a central dust-collection system. For the table saw, the connecting ductwork can be run from the collector across the ceiling, then down a shop wall close to the machine. Where the duct meets the floor, you can connect a length of flexible hose to the duct work with a quick disconnect fitting. It is then easy enough to move the hose out of the way when the need arises.

For more information on setting up dust-collection systems, see *Fine Woodworking #67* and *Woodshop Dust Control* by Sandor Nagyszalanczy (The Taunton Press, 1996).

Shop Accessories

Several accessories will make your table saw easier to use. Some, such as auxiliary supports, are virtually essential; others, such as carts and storage racks, are enormously helpful. Below are some of the setups I've developed in my many years as a woodworker.

AUXILIARY SUPPORTS

Auxiliary supports increase the working surface of the table saw, carrying long or wide workpieces at the tabletop height. Outfeed supports are a necessary safety feature because most table saws provide less than 6 in. of support behind the blade. You definitely don't want to be reaching over the blade to prevent a piece from falling after the cut. An auxiliary side table supports the edges of panels when making wide cuts.

Auxiliary supports can take many forms, ranging from a simple set of sawhorses spanned by a piece of sheet material to plastic-laminated extension tables projecting from the rear and right side of the saw. Workbenches are about the same height as the saw table, so I have used mine many times as an outfeed-support surface.

Fold-down tables and steel-roller systems that attach to the rear of the saw are convenient for a small shop because they drop out of the way when not in use. (see Sources on p. 197). You can also buy roller stands as separate units, but I have found that if these are not aligned at exactly 90 degrees to the blade, they tend to steer the workpiece to one side or the other.

If you have the room, a large extension-table system is much better when it comes to handling large workpieces. Biesemeyer offers two laminated outfeed-support tables—one "professional" size and one for the home shop—that are designed to attach to the back rail of a Biesemeyer fence system. The tables are adjustable in height and come with milled slots to accommodate an extended miter-gauge bar or jig runners (see the top photo on p. 110). The extra table area is also useful for drawing and assembly work. I keep it waxed to resist glue.

Of course, you can make your own extension tables instead of buying them. Attach a two-legged extension table to the saw table with clamps or with brackets through the guide rails. Alternatively, build a freestanding four-legged table. An outfeed support should be at the same height, or slightly below, the saw table (see the photo at left). A side extension table should be at exactly the same height as the saw tabletop.

CARTS

Wheeled carts or tables can be used for moving lumber from machine to machine or for holding project parts as you are processing them (see the photo at left on the facing page). When working at the table saw, I find it more convenient and safer to work from a stack of parts on a cart rather than piling things on the saw table. Parts stacked neatly on a cart are easy to count and missed joints are clearly evident.

Carts are easy to obtain. You can get them at furniture-factory auctions or you can recycle food carts from hospital junk piles. You can also build your own or make one by attaching casters to an old table. It is useful to have some carts that are low to the floor and some at bench height.

RACKS, DRUMS, BOXES, AND BUCKETS

In a well-organized workspace, frequently used table-saw tools and accessories are kept within reach of the saw. These include your push sticks, arbor wrenches, miter gauge, fences, throat plates, guards, maintenance supplies, and featherboards. You might also want to store your sawblades, jigs, clipboard, and patterns nearby.

Some saws come equipped with brackets for holding the accessories that you use the most—the rip fence and miter gauge, as well as the arbor wrench. If your saw didn't come with brackets, they are easy enough to make.

Since a set of good sawblades can easily cost more than your table saw, it makes sense to take good care of them. I made a simple wall-hung saw-

Setting Up Extension Rollers

If extension rollers aren't set perfectly perpendicular to the sawblade, they can steer a workpiece out of line while feeding it.

An extension should be at the saw height or slightly below the saw table. Some tables can fold down out of the way when necessary.

Wheeled carts can conveniently ferry workpieces and work in process from machine to machine. A cart can also serve as an extension table when needed.

A simple wall-hung box keeps blades organized and separated to protect them from damaging each other.

blade box to protect my blades while keeping them at the ready (see the photo at right above). I keep my collection of pushers on top of this box.

Large 55-gallon drums are handy for holding wood scraps or sawdust. With a panel placed across the top, they can be used as temporary parts tables. A drum is also a handy place to set the rip fence if you have to remove it from the saw temporarily—better than the floor, where it's likely to get damaged or tripped over. A scrap box or bucket next to the saw (not that I always hit it) helps control the mess from cutoffs. Pieces in the bucket either go into the 55-gallon drums or serve as fuel for the wood-stove. Larger pieces go to my scrap shelves if I think they can be used later.

Tools at the Table Saw

There are two types of important tools I keep by the table saw: layout tools for measuring, marking, and checking the workpiece, and tools for setting up the table-saw blade, miter gauge, and rip fence for various cuts. You will be repaid many times over by investing in good tools and keeping them in good condition. Good tools enhance accuracy, and the more accurate your work at the table saw, the better your projects will turn out.

Squares and rulers are the tools that you'll probably use the most at the table saw. You'll need a 6-in. try square to check fence and miter-gauge setups and the ends of your crosscuts. A machinist's combination square is handy for checking 45-degree miters and for gauging lines, as when used as a marking gauge. A framing square is useful for layout and square reference on larger panels and as a straightedge for confirming flatness.

Handy Square

I like to carry a 2-in. engineer's square in my shop apron for checking edges.

Sliding Bevel

Use a sliding bevel for checking and marking angles other than 90 degrees on the workpiece, the blade, and the miter gauge. A gauge with the locking nut at the end of the handle is more versatile than one with a wing nut on the side at the head.

DRESSING FOR SUCCESS

I LEARNED TO WEAR A SHOP APRON FROM MY WIFE, who looks unkindly at saw-dust and wood chips hanging precariously off my clothes when I come into the house. Of course, a shop apron serves other purposes besides protecting my clothes and marriage. The apron's breast and waist pockets hold the tools that I use the most at the table saw: a pencil, a 6-in. ruler, a 2-in. engineer's square, and 4-in. sliding calipers.

Shop aprons are reasonably priced at hardware and discount stores, and you can probably order a dozen aprons at a time even more cheaply. Even though I wash my aprons, the glue that ultimately cakes on them forces me to throw them out, so I'm glad for the ones kept in reserve.

Check each square periodically for accuracy by placing it against the straight edge of a board and marking a line with a sharp pencil. Flip the square on the same edge and check the blade's alignment with the mark. Any deviation from 90 degrees will be doubled.

I usually carry a 6-in. metal precision ruler with metric measurements on one side and English measurements (inches) on the other. The metric measurements come in handy for calculations because they allow for finer gradations and don't involve fractions. The pocket rule will take care of much of the close work done at the saw.

For longer measurements, I find that both a folding rule and a short tape measure have their own advantages. The tape measure hooks onto the end of a board, making it easy to take long measurements. A rigid folding rule is easier to handle and is better for the more exacting work of marking joinery. Because rulers often vary from each other, it's best to use only one ruler on a job. You can check your ruler for accuracy with a machinist's rule.

A 4-in. sliding caliper with metric and English measurements is handy for checking stock thickness and narrow widths. The caliper can be used for inside and outside measurements and is more precise than measuring with a ruler.

Pencils are essential marking tools. I keep a #2 pencil behind my ear or in the top pocket of my apron. A carpenter's pencil or beginner's #308 school pencil with a thick lead is best for marking wood in the milling stage. Save your thin-lead pencils for writing, sketching, and marking joints.

Masking tape is indispensable in the woodshop. A few of its myriad uses include marking on the table-saw surface for rough cutoffs, leveling the throat plate, keeping small parts together, shimming jigs, fences, and stops that are a smidgen out of square, and taping back chips until you can glue them back in.

Ripping

R ipping and crosscutting are the most basic and common operations performed on the table saw. Ripping is sawing with the
grain—in other words, along the length of a board. Crosscutting is
sawing across the grain of the wood. The two operations are fundamen-
tally distinct and require different cutting approaches.

In this chapter, I'll discuss techniques for safe and accurate ripping of
solid wood and sheet stock. I'll address crosscutting in the next chapter.

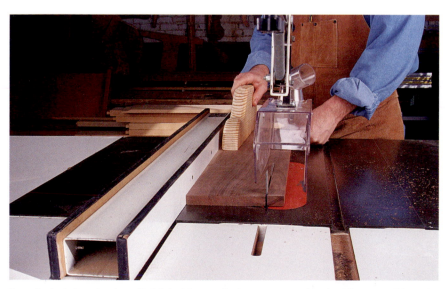

For a typical rip cut, a board's jointed face and edge are pressed against the saw table and
fence. The operator stands to the side of the board and finishes the cut using a pusher.

Preparing Wood

For safe work, a piece of wood ideally should be prepared with one straight edge and one flat face. The straight edge, which rides against the fence, prevents the board from binding between the fence and the blade. The flat face, which rides on the saw table, keeps the workpiece from rocking while being fed through the blade.

A workpiece that doesn't ride firmly against the fence and table is an invitation for dangerous kickback (see the sidebar on p. 65). Kickback can be eliminated by using a properly aligned splitter or riving knife, but I'm forced to acknowledge that many woodworkers don't currently use one. I want to reiterate here that I don't recommend using a table saw without a splitter or riving knife!

The easiest way to straighten an edge and flatten a face is to run the workpiece over a jointer. If you don't have a jointer, you can handplane the stock or buy surfaced lumber from most suppliers. If an edge is extremely irregular, like that on a rough-cut slab, it's much faster to saw the edge than to joint it. One approach is to strike a straight line, cut to it using a bandsaw, then finish straightening the edge on a jointer or with a handplane.

Alternatively, you can attach a straight-edged guide to one edge of the slab, then run the guide against the fence (see the illustration below). You'll now have a straight edge on your workpiece that you can run against the fence. Another way to rip irregular stock is to use a sled that secures the work at the front against a wooden stop (see the top photo on the facing page). If you have a European saw, you can also rip a board using the sliding table (see the bottom photo on the facing page).

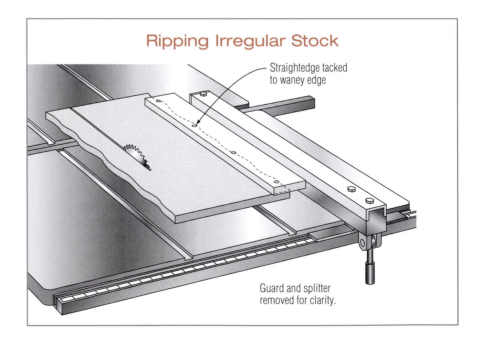

Ripping Irregular Stock

Straightedge tacked to waney edge

Guard and splitter removed for clarity.

To rip irregular stock, you can place the stock on a panel jig guided by a runner in a miter-gauge slot. The front end of the stock is pressed against a stop that's screwed to the leading end of the jig. Snipped-off brads projecting from the stop prevent the board from slipping. The trailing end is held down firmly against the sled.

The sliding table on a European saw can be used to rip irregular stock. The leading end of the stock gets jammed under an angled plate at the end of the sliding table.

RIPPING AN UNSURFACED BOARD

It's not always possible or desirable to joint and thickness-plane stock before ripping. For example, jointing a wide board to remove a large cup or twist often leaves the board too thin for your purposes. In that case, it's best to rip the pieces to rough width before jointing. That way, there's much less cup to remove on the jointer.

WOOD OFTEN CONTAINS STRESSES THAT ARE RELIEVED when a board is cut. So-called reactive wood can spread apart or pinch together as it's being ripped. This can cause the board to bind between the blade and the fence, causing dangerous kickback if you don't have a splitter or riving knife.

One way to prevent reactive wood from binding is to allow room behind the blade for the workpiece to spread out. To accomplish this on a European saw, you can slide the fence toward you and lock it in place so that it ends at the front of the blade. (The Unifence will also do this, as discussed on p. 35.) If your fence doesn't have this sliding fore-and-aft adjustment, you can outfit your fence with a half-fence to serve the same purpose.

A half-fence is easy to make (see the illustration at right below). Use a stable material such as maple or good-quality hardwood plywood. Applying a plastic laminate face will reduce feed friction. The fence should be taller than the thickest stock your blade will handle. Like all auxiliary fences, the half-fence should include a ⅛-in. by ⅛-in. rabbet along the bottom edge to prevent sawdust and small chips from lodging between the workpiece and fence.

You can make a simple stationary fence that clamps or bolts to your rip fence with the end of the half-fence extending about 1 in. beyond the forward gullets. But a sliding half-fence, like that shown in the photos at right, works better because you can fine-tune its position. Ideally, the end of a half-fence should extend 1 in. past the gullets at the front of the blade. Because the position of the gullets varies with the height of the blade, a sliding fence allows for the necessary fore-and-aft adjustment. The cove at the leading end of the fence accommodates varying thicknesses of stock to some degree, minimizing necessary fore-and-aft adjustments.

Using a half-fence can feel a bit awkward at first because the workpiece is unsupported once it passes the blade, but you get used to the process pretty quickly.

A half-fence, which extends just beyond the cutting edge of the sawblade, allows the workpiece to spread apart after being cut, reducing the risk of kickback.

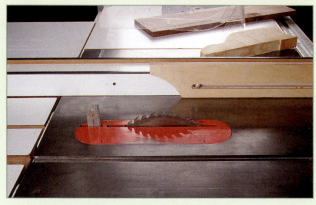

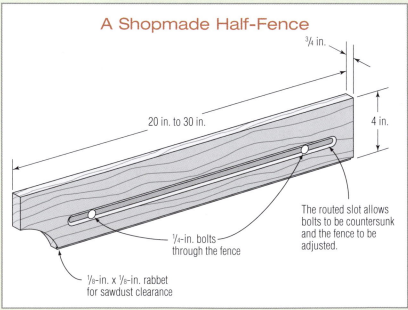

A Shopmade Half-Fence

¾ in.

20 in. to 30 in.

4 in.

¼-in. bolts through the fence

The routed slot allows bolts to be countersunk and the fence to be adjusted.

⅛-in. x ⅛-in. rabbet for sawdust clearance

The safest way to rip unsurfaced stock is to use a bandsaw, but it can be done on a table saw. Unfortunately, ripping a warped board on a table saw can be dangerous, especially without using a splitter or riving knife, even when the stock has a straight edge for riding against the fence. A cupped board fed through the blade with the concave side down is fairly stable until it reaches the end of the cut, when it can collapse, pinching between the blade and the fence.

On the other hand, if a board is fed with the concave side up, it won't collapse at the end of the cut but it can rock from side to side while being cut. Of the two approaches, I favor the former. Even though the workpiece can collapse at the end of the cut, a splitter or riving knife can prevent it from being thrown backward. A half-fence is useful here too (see the sidebar on the facing page), as is ripping with a sliding table.

Basic Ripping Techniques

The standard procedure for ripping a board involves selecting the blade, setting its height, setting the fence, then making the cut with a blade cover and splitter or riving knife in place. Your stance at the saw is also critical to safety and accuracy.

SETTING THE BLADE HEIGHT

The blade-height setting has an effect upon feed resistance, heat generation, and exit tearout. On the one hand, the higher the blade, the less feed resistance and the cooler the blade runs. On the other hand, a high blade presents more danger and produces more tearout on the bottom of the cut. It can also produce more forceful kickback if you're not using a splitter or riving knife. (Again, I don't recommend sawing without one!)

However, if you don't have a splitter or riving knife on your saw, set the blade about ⅛ in. above the top of the workpiece. With a sharp blade and a properly tuned saw, the benefits of setting the blade high are minimal. Ask me how high to set the blade and I'm likely to ask you how deeply you want to cut into your fingers.

If you're using a blade cover and a splitter or riving knife, you can safely set the blade as high as you like. For the most efficient chip removal, set your blade so that the primary blade gullets clear the top of the workpiece.

SETTING THE FENCE

Move the rip fence in position for the desired width of cut. For accuracy and safety, it's critical that the fence be parallel to the blade or cocked just a hair away at the rear of the blade. If you have a premium rip fence that's adjusted properly, it should stay properly aligned to the blade regardless of the fence's position on its rail. However, if you have an old-style fence, you'll probably need to check parallelism to the blade for

Blades for Ripping

When initially ripping a number of boards to rough width at the beginning of a project, I recommend using a 24-tooth FTG blade. This blade is designed to cut easily through stock, even thick hardwoods. The rough edge left by a 24-tooth blade is not an issue because you can rip workpieces to final size later using a good-quality 40-tooth ATB blade, which leaves a much smoother edge.

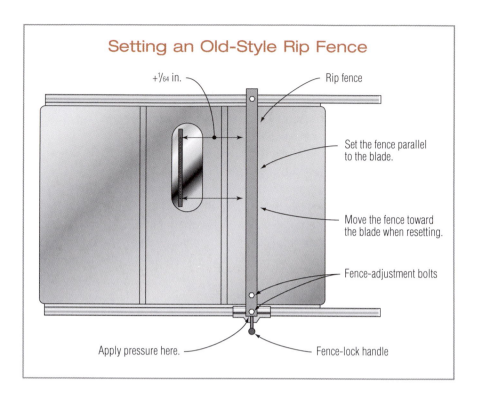

Setting an Old-Style Rip Fence

+1/64 in.

Rip fence

Set the fence parallel to the blade.

Move the fence toward the blade when resetting.

Fence-adjustment bolts

Apply pressure here.

Fence-lock handle

every cut, since these fences are notorious for locking to the rail at a slight angle to the blade.

To set an old-style fence for a cut, begin by moving it toward the blade rather than away from it. This helps prevent the drag on the rear fence rail from cocking the rear of the fence toward the blade. While moving the fence, push the front sleeve against the rail to help keep the fence square to the rail, then lock the fence in place (see the illustration above). After locking the fence, double-check your setup by measuring from your fence to both the front and rear of the blade.

When setting the fence for your width of cut, you can use the cursor and scale on a premium fence, or you can measure the distance between the fence and blade using an accurate ruler. Sometimes, you may want to use a previously cut workpiece to set the fence.

MAKING THE CUT

Put on your safety gear, ensure that the blade cover is working properly, and see that the saw table is free of debris. Make sure your splitter or riving knife is aligned properly to prevent kickback (see the sidebar on the facing page). Whenever possible, orient the workpiece with its finished, or outside, face up so that any tearout takes place on the underside.

Turn on the saw and allow the blade to reach full speed. Place the workpiece on the table with its straight edge against the fence, and move the stock into the blade. Feed the work through the blade at a steady rate, pushing it about as fast as the saw will cut. The proper feed rate is deter-

Licking Kickback

THE DANGER OF KICKBACK IS CONSTANTLY LURKING AT THE TABLE SAW. No matter how perfectly your fence is aligned and how carefully you feed a workpiece, the rising rear teeth of the blade may pick up the workpiece, hurling it at you at fierce speeds. The only sure way to prevent kickback is to use a properly aligned splitter or riving knife. I don't cut without one. If you don't like the inconvenient stock splitter that came with your table saw, there are several aftermarket models available (see "Splitters and Riving Knives" on p. 67).

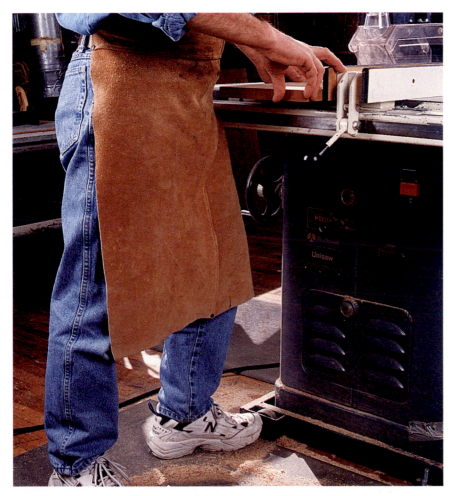

To maximize stability when ripping, stand at the front of the saw to the left of the blade with your left foot in contact with the base and your hip against the front rail.

mined by the type of blade, the power of the saw, and the density of the wood. Feeding too slowly can overheat the blade and burn the workpiece, whereas feeding too fast can strain the motor on an underpowered saw. Listen to the saw as you cut. If the motor slows down as you cut, feed a bit more slowly.

Be sure to pay attention to your stance when ripping. It's dangerous to stand back from the table saw because the farther away you are, the more you have to overreach to make the cut. This is awkward and can throw you off-balance. The correct approach is to stand at the front of the saw to the left of the blade with your left foot in contact with the base and your hip against the front rail (see the photo on p. 129). In this position, the saw helps to stabilize your body, leaving your arms free to manipulate the work. Keep your right arm in line with the workpiece being pushed along the fence to the right of the blade. At the end of the cut, you'll be in a comfortable, balanced position.

It's wise to use a pusher when ripping stock that's less than 8 in. wide between the blade and the fence. A pusher acts as an extension of your hand, giving you added control as well as an extra measure of safety. (For more on pushers, see p. 79).

When ripping, pay close attention to where the workpiece meets the fence, not the blade. Keep the workpiece against the fence for the entirety of the cut. You can use your left hand to apply light pressure to push the workpiece against the fence in front of the blade. (Keep your left hand stationary on the saw table well in front of the blade. As soon as the work-

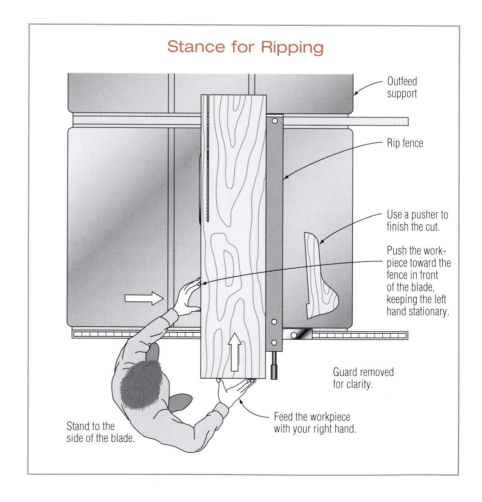

Stance for Ripping

Outfeed support

Rip fence

Use a pusher to finish the cut.

Push the work-piece toward the fence in front of the blade, keeping the left hand stationary.

Guard removed for clarity.

Stand to the side of the blade.

Feed the workpiece with your right hand.

piece passes, remove your hand from the saw table.) As the cut comes to an end, use a pusher in your right hand to hold the work down and against the fence (see the illustration on the facing page).

Ripping Long Stock

As you rip, you need some form of outfeed support, even if it's just a short outfeed table. When ripping long boards, additional support is necessary. I always use a long extension table, but if you don't have one, you can use an auxiliary support stand or a human helper.

Auxiliary supports can be freestanding or fixed to the saw. Commercial units of various sorts are available, but you can just as easily make auxiliary supports yourself. A sawhorse set at the proper height will serve, but an extension table is much more useful (for more on auxiliary supports, see p. 119).

A helper, or tail-off person, who understands how a table saw operates can make cutting long boards safer and more efficient. The helper is a human support stand who can also return the work to you. A helper should never pull on a board, but simply support it with both hands from underneath. It's up to the operator, not the helper, to guide the board (see the photo below). After each board is cut, the helper can stack the workpieces and either dispense with the offcut or push it back to the operator for further cutting. Working together, the saw operator and a helper can develop a rhythm for efficient, safe cutting.

(for more on auxiliary supports, see p. 119).

Long-Board Strategy

When you are cutting just a few long boards, a support stand or outfeed table will do, but if you have a lot of long boards to cut, get a helper if possible.

When you are ripping a lot of long stock, using a helper to accept the boards can be very efficient. The helper should never pull or guide a board, but simply support it with palms upraised.

Before ripping a long board, always prepare one straight edge and one flat face. Keep your pusher on the saw table near the fence so it's at the ready when you need it. Line up an outfeed support to receive the cut pieces.

Begin by propping the board against the saw, then turning on the machine. Holding the trailing end of the board in your right hand, lift it slightly to ensure that the leading end of the board contacts the tabletop. Place your left hand as far forward on the edge as you comfortably can to apply diagonal pressure to keep the board against the fence. Walk the board forward until its end reaches the saw table, then grab a pusher to complete the cut (see the photos below).

When ripping long boards, hold the end of the board in your right hand, with your left hand extended as far forward as comfortably possible. Lift the rear end of the board slightly and walk forward, keeping the board against the fence. Move right up against the saw to finish the cut.

Ripping Sheet Stock

I don't use plywood or other man-made boards very much in my work, but there are times when I need to rip sheet stock—for example, when building jigs or doing utility work around the shop. Ripping sheet stock refers to cutting pieces to width using the rip fence. The two biggest challenges when cutting sheet stock concern maneuverability and tearout. I'll talk about maneuverability first.

Feeding full-sized 4-ft. by 8-ft. sheets across a table saw can be unwieldy. It demands use of auxiliary supports or a helper because the material is often either heavy or thin and floppy. You should place sturdy auxiliary supports at almost the level of the saw's tabletop. When dealing with wide offcuts, you'll need side support as well as infeed and outfeed supports.

An extended fence can also help when cutting sheet goods by providing more bearing surface against the fence (see the illustration below). You may need to clamp down the rear end of the fence to resist the increased sideways pressure.

The thin face veneers on many sheet goods are particularly prone to tearout. You can minimize this by using the proper blade (see chapter 3). Also, a zero-clearance throat plate will provide maximum backup on the exit side of the cut (see "The Throat Plate" on p. 98). Of course, it's wise to place the "show" side of the workpiece up because the cut on the top side will be cleaner.

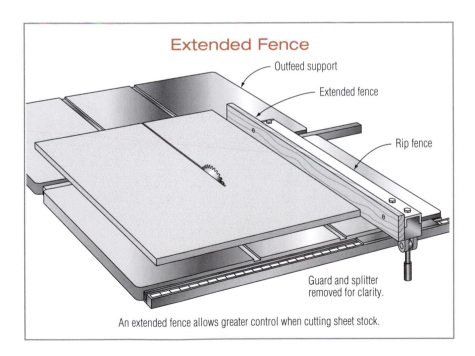

Extended Fence

Outfeed support

Extended fence

Rip fence

Guard and splitter removed for clarity.

An extended fence allows greater control when cutting sheet stock.

Ripping Sheet Goods

RIPPING FULL-SIZE SHEET GOODS can be challenging. To make it easier on yourself, use outfeed supports and approach the process as shown here.

1 Begin the process of ripping a sheet by bracing it against the front of the saw table.

2 Standing at the rear left corner of the sheet, walk the piece forward while applying pressure diagonally against the fence in front of the blade.

3 Maintaining pressure against the fence, walk the sheet forward until the saw is bearing the entire weight of the sheet.

4 Move around to the rear of the sheet, with your right hand centered between the blade and the fence. Push straight forward to complete the cut.

The Importance of a Good Rip Fence

THE IMPORTANCE OF A GOOD RIP FENCE CANNOT BE OVERSTATED. A fence that is straight and that firmly locks parallel to the blade makes all the difference when it comes to safe, accurate, efficient ripping. As discussed on p. 37, many new fence systems are available to replace old-style sheet-metal fences that tend to have bowed faces and that often don't lock parallel to the blade.

One fix for a bowed fence is to outfit it with an auxiliary fence. The auxiliary fence—made from a straight piece of plywood or straight-grained hardwood—can be bolted or clamped to the rip fence (see the illustration below). If necessary, shim behind the auxiliary fence to straighten it or square it to your saw table. A ⅛-in. by ⅛-in. rabbet along the bottom edge serves as an escape chute for chips and sawdust that might otherwise get trapped between the fence and workpiece.

Just as important as the type of fence is its proper alignment to the blade. An improperly adjusted fence invites kickback and burning of the stock. Make sure that your fence is properly adjusted before you rip any wood (see "Adjusting the Rip Fence" on p. 105).

Practice Feeding Sheet Goods

When learning to cut sheet goods, you may find that it helps to lower the blade below the table and practice feeding a sheet before making the actual cut.

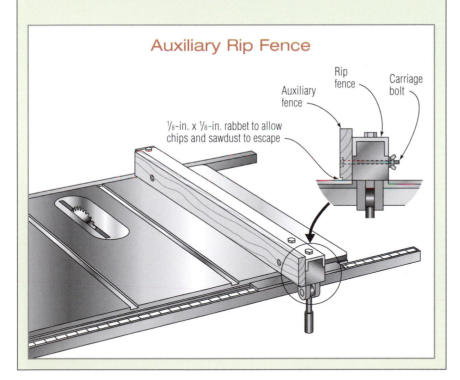

Auxiliary Rip Fence

⅛-in. x ⅛-in. rabbet to allow chips and sawdust to escape

Auxiliary fence

Rip fence

Carriage bolt

If the work is fragile (a fine laminate, for example) and you're experiencing tearout at the bottom of the cut, try making a preliminary pass with the blade set for a very shallow scoring cut. This will slice the fibers clean, and there should be no tearout when the piece is cut through. If you work a lot with sheet goods, consider using a scoring blade, as discussed on p. 58.

When cutting sheet stock, you generally stand much farther to the left of the blade than when ripping solid wood. The best place to stand to rip a panel is at its far left rear corner. From there, you can guide the piece in a straight line along the fence, pushing forward at the same time. With your left hand, grasp the left outside edge about 1 ft. from the corner. Place your right hand on the rear edge, with your arm extended (see the photos on p. 134).

Begin the cut by walking the sheet forward, maintaining pressure against the fence in front of the blade. Do not apply sideways pressure once the blade has entered the workpiece. As you approach the saw, shift your body closer to the line of cut. Position your right hand on the rear edge of the sheet between the blade and the fence. Move your left hand closer to the corner, where it will help keep the sheet against the fence in front of the blade. As the cut comes to an end, slightly reduce the forward pressure of your left hand to prevent cocking the offcut into the blade.

Cutting a 4-ft. by 8-ft. sheet can be challenging, but as long as you have auxiliary supports properly set up and you feed the work as described, you'll do fine.

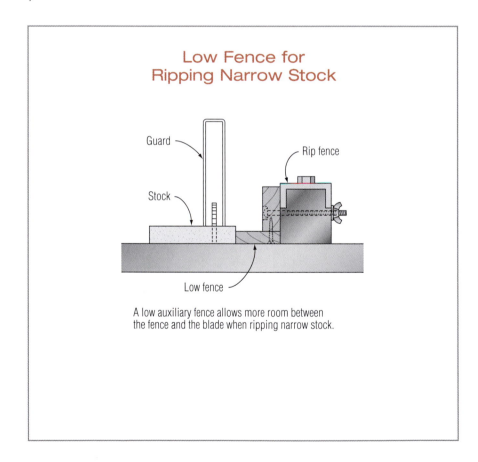

Low Fence for Ripping Narrow Stock

Guard

Rip fence

Stock

Low fence

A low auxiliary fence allows more room between the fence and the blade when ripping narrow stock.

Ripping Narrow Stock

The difficulty in ripping narrow stock is the fence's proximity to the blade and blade cover. When ripping very narrow stock, there is very little space between the fence and the blade cover in which to manipulate a pusher, and many blade covers impede the process.

As a result, many woodworkers remove the blade cover and splitter to rip narrow pieces. However, it's a dangerous mistake to work without the protection of these devices. There are safe ways to rip narrow stock with the cover and splitter in place.

First, if the piece you need is at least 2 in. wide, you can attach an L-shaped auxiliary fence to your rip fence (see the illustration on the facing page). The additional space that the fence provides allows more room for your hand and pusher.

You can also make a simple jig for ripping workpieces that are less than 2 in. wide. The jig is nothing more than a straight piece of wood with a handle on top and a stop on the side (see the illustration below). This jig works well for pieces that aren't very long, because the jig needs to be almost as long as the stock being cut. To use the jig, place the stock against the edge of the jig and the stop at its end. Hold the jig's handle in your right hand while using a pusher in your left hand to steady the

Jig for Ripping Narrrow Stock

Guard and splitter removed for clarity.

Jig

The workpiece rests against the stop.

workpiece against the jig. When ripping very narrow pieces, use a zero-clearance throat insert to prevent the rippings from falling into the blade opening (see the sidebar on p. 99).

A third alternative is to use a box-style blade cover such as the Brett-Guard (see the photo on p. 62). Unlike basket-style covers, the underside of one edge of the Brett-Guard is scalloped, so the blade can be set right at the edge of the cover for ripping narrow stock. By using a pusher that is thinner than the space between the blade and the fence, you can rip stock as thin as ⅛ in.

One final way to safely rip narrow stock is to saw it from the outer edge of the stock, rather than from the edge that rides against the fence. This technique doesn't work well for multiples of the same size though, since it requires resetting the fence for every cut.

Ripping Short Pieces

Trying to rip a short piece of wood is asking for trouble because the wood may not reach the splitter or riving knife before the end of the cut, so it can be easily thrown. Ideally, short pieces should be cut to length from longer rippings, but that's not always practical. The best way that I've found to safely rip short pieces is with a cutoff box, using a hold-down (see the photo below).

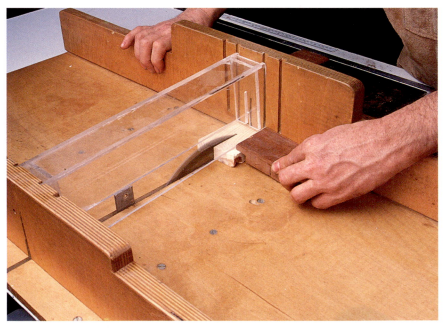

If it's not practical to rip short pieces from longer rippings, secure the short pieces in a crosscut sled using a hold-down.

Ripping Thin Stock

Ripping stock that is ⅛ in. thick or less requires a pusher with a shallow heel and a sole that is long enough to keep the piece from lifting up onto the blade as it is being cut. Some people use featherboards or safety wheels to hold down the workpieces, but I find that they just get in the way. An appropriate pusher will hold the work flat for the entirety of the cut.

If your rip fence doesn't closely meet the saw table, the workpiece can creep under it. To prevent that, attach an auxiliary fence that sits tightly against the table. Outfeed support also helps when handling thin, floppy material.

Ripping Thick Stock

The thicker the workpiece, the harder the saw has to work to cut through it. When ripping thick stock, use a 24-tooth FTG blade, as discussed in chapter 3. As you cut, listen to the saw motor and adjust your feed rate accordingly. As with other ripping operations, feed the stock as quickly as possible without bogging down the motor. If you encounter stiff resistance even when using a sharp FTG blade, try using a thin-kerf blade, which cuts easier because it's removing less wood (see the sidebar on p. 47).

If the workpiece is thicker than the cutting capacity of the blade, make one cut from one side, then flip the board over to complete the cut (see the photos on p. 140). Pay careful attention to feed speed when making the first cut. Because the blade is totally buried in the wood, chip ejection is less efficient and the blade can run hotter. Make the cut as quickly as possible without taxing the motor.

Standing at Ease

MY FIRST SHOP HAD A CONCRETE FLOOR, and it didn't take too many hours of standing to appreciate the relief that a rubber mat afforded. Although I'm fortunate to have wood shop floors now, I still stand on a rubber mat at the table saw, as well as at other machines. These mats greatly reduce leg fatigue and provide a nonslip surface among the sawdust and shavings on the floor. (For suppliers of rubber mats, see Sources on p. 197.)

A good pair of shoes also goes a long way toward keeping your legs and feet from developing problems. When standing in one place for long periods, worn-out or cheaply made shoes can be a real pain.

In addition to standing on a mat and wearing good shoes, it sometimes helps to adjust your vertical position at the saw for more comfort. For example, when cutting a lot of finger joints, I've found that standing on a low plywood platform helps reduce leg fatigue by raising me up to a more comfortable position for this tedious operation.

If the thickness of a workpiece exceeds the capacity of your blade, rip the piece in two opposing passes. To prevent kickback, I use a Delta Disappearing Splitter with the fingers removed. Instead, you could use a shopmade splitter, as shown in the sidebar on p. 68. To make the second cut, flip the board end-for-end, raising the blade only as much as necessary.

Resawing

Resawing means sawing a piece of work on edge to yield two or more thinner pieces. Sometimes woodworkers will resaw by making opposing cuts into the edges of a workpiece, as described on p. 139. This is very dangerous because the buried blade can overheat or bind, a blade cover can't be used, and balancing the workpiece can be awkward. Because of the dangers involved, I strongly discourage resawing on a table saw. Use a bandsaw instead.

Ripping Angles

There are times when you need to rip a board at an angle—that is, not parallel to the edge of a workpiece. Cutting tapered legs is a common example of this. There are also times when you may want the grain on a board angled in a particular way for appearance or strength. Sometimes, you may need to make an angled cut to avoid a bow or defect in a plank, or you may be able to get more yield from a board by ripping it at an angle.

To rip a board at an angle, secure it with hold-downs to a sled that either rides in the saw's miter-gauge slots (see the photo below) or against the rip fence. The hold-downs are adjustable across the sled's width, allowing you to hold work safely at almost any angle.

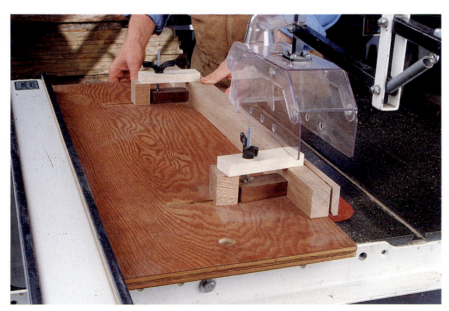

Tapers can be cut safely using a sled with adjustable hold-downs.

Rip in One Pass if Possible

When you are ripping thick stock, it may be tempting to make a series of shallow, multiple passes. However, this is not a good idea because the workpiece can distort in the process, yielding a bad cut.

Always rip bevels with the blade tilted away from the fence and the finished workpiece (not the offcut) riding against the fence. For right-tilt saws, the fence will usually have to be positioned to the left of the blade.

Ripping Bevels

Sawing a bevel along the grain is similar to standard ripping except that the blade is tilted at an angle other than 90 degrees. To avoid kickback and burning and to get the cleanest cut possible, be sure to angle the blade away from the fence and use a splitter or riving knife. The cut piece you want to save should always ride along the fence, with the beveled edge above the tilted blade (see the photo above). If you trap it under the blade and against the fence, it can burn and kick back. Most table saws tilt to the right, meaning you'll need to work with the fence on the left side of the blade.

Crosscutting

Crosscutting means sawing wood to length across the grain. Wood is generally crosscut after it has been ripped to width. The workpiece is fed crosswise into the blade, guided by a miter gauge, crosscut sled, or sliding table.

For the most part, crosscutting is a less dangerous operation than ripping. Since the workpiece isn't confined between the blade and the fence, there is little danger of it kicking back. With miter-gauge cutting, the danger lies with the offcut that's left near the blade, where it's prone to be thrown. As with ripping, the splitter and blade guard are important safeguards.

Guiding the Workpiece

Just as the rip fence is necessary to guide a workpiece when ripping, you'll need a safe and accurate method of guiding a workpiece when crosscutting. The two most common accessories for crosscutting are the miter gauge and the crosscut sled. In this section, I'll discuss how to best modify a stock miter gauge for effective crosscutting and how to make a crosscut sled. I'll also address crosscutting with a sliding or rolling table.

MITER GAUGES
The miter gauge is guided by a metal bar that slides in slots machined in the table-saw top parallel to the sawblade (see "Miter Gauge and Miter Slots" on p. 38). The body of the gauge, which can be set to any angle

One of the best ways to crosscut a board to length is to use a crosscut sled that slides in your saw's miter-gauge slots. The sled is much more stable and accurate than a stock miter gauge.

from 30 degrees to 90 degrees, guides the workpiece as it's pushed through the blade.

For most crosscutting operations, I find the stock miter gauge inaccurate and awkward because of its small body and single guide bar. The truth is, I hardly ever use a miter gauge. However, if you do, the best improvement you can make to your stock miter gauge is to add an auxiliary fence, which will provide an increased bearing surface for the workpiece, stabilizing it during the cut (see the top sidebar on the facing page).

One safety problem when using a miter gauge is that small offcuts tend to gather around the sawblade as you make repeated cuts. These pieces can be easily thrown if they contact the spinning blade. If the offcuts are very thin, they can also wedge into the throat-plate opening, catching the workpiece and possibly lifting the throat plate in the process. The best solution here is to use a splitter or riving knife and a zero-clearance throat plate. Additionally, you can make an auxiliary fence that extends past the sawblade to support the pieces and carry them past the danger zone (see

Making an Auxiliary Miter-Gauge Fence

MAKE YOUR AUXILIARY FENCE FROM ¾-IN.-THICK, stable, straight-grained stock with two parallel faces. The fence can be any length, but 24 in. seems to work fine for most operations. As with any auxiliary fence, cut a ⅛-in. by ⅛-in. rabbet along its bottom edge as a clearance chute for sawdust and chips.

A piece of sandpaper attached to the fence face with contact cement will help prevent the workpiece from slipping. This is particularly useful when making miter cuts, which tend to push the workpiece away from the blade.

Screw the auxiliary fence to the miter gauge through two predrilled holes in the miter-gauge body. Position the fence on the gauge so that the first cut will trim off the end of the fence. That way, you can use the end of the fence as a reference for cutlines.

Auxiliary Miter-Gauge Fence

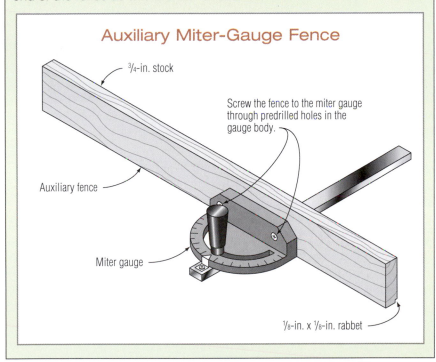

³/₄-in. stock

Screw the fence to the miter gauge through predrilled holes in the gauge body.

Auxiliary fence

Miter gauge

⅛-in. x ⅛-in. rabbet

Replacement Miter Gauges

THE INADEQUACIES OF STANDARD MITER GAUGES have led to the development of a number of aftermarket replacement miter gauges. Most of these gauges, which range in price from about $50 to $150, have a long body to provide greater support for the workpiece. The fence is typically an aluminum extrusion, which is adjustable to provide support right up to the blade at any angle. Some systems have adjustable drop-stops that make setting up for repetitive crosscutting easier and more efficient. Many of these features are standard on miter gauges that come with some European table saws.

Small Sled for Small Pieces

Although a large crosscut sled can handle small pieces, a smaller sled made for that purpose is easier and more convenient to operate.

An auxiliary fence that extends past the blade will push cutoffs past the blade so they can't be thrown at the operator. Sandpaper attached to the fence prevents workpiece slippage.

the photo above). To prevent cutting off the end of the fence, you'll need to make the fence taller than the workpiece being cut.

CROSSCUT SLEDS

Years ago, after I struggled with large workpieces supported only by an aux-iliary fence on my miter gauge, it dawned on me that there had to be a better way to make accurate crosscuts. And so was born the first of my crosscut sleds.

A crosscut sled is basically a panel with runners that slide in the table saw's miter-gauge slots. A fence on the operator's side of the panel guides the workpiece. A rail at the rear simply serves to hold the two halves of the sled together there. For safety, a clear Lexan blade cover fits between the fence and rear rail, and a rear exit guard covers the blade where it exits the fence. You'll be thrilled at how easily and accurately you can cut work-pieces using a crosscut sled.

It's not difficult to make a crosscut sled (see the sidebar on pp. 148–149). My first sled was made primarily to handle wide workpieces such as table-tops and chest sides. However, much crosscutting and joinery done at the table saw involves fairly narrow pieces, so you can make scaled-down sleds, which are easier to handle.

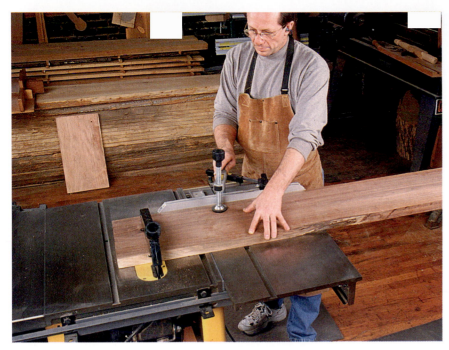

A sliding table—like the one on this DeWalt® 746 saw—allows easy, accurate crosscutting of long, wide, or heavy workpieces.

A number of crosscut sleds are available commercially if you choose not to make one. These sleds include a variety of features including drop-stops and adjustable fences that can be angled for miter cuts (see Sources on p. 197).

SLIDING TABLES

These days, I do all of my crosscutting—particularly of larger pieces—using the sliding table on my European table saw. A sliding table allows accurate, safe, effortless crosscutting because it is solid, precisely machined, and it nestles right up to the sawblade (see the photo above). A sliding table, which is integral to the saw itself, should not be confused with aftermarket rolling tables, which I'll discuss in the next section.

A sliding table is particularly useful when it comes to crosscutting sheet goods and other wide panels, but it's also great for crosscutting long, thick stock. The fence on a sliding table can easily be adjusted to any angle for sawing miters or compound bevels on the ends of workpieces. Many fences include drop-stops for convenient repetitive cutting. (For more on sliding tables, see "European Saws" on p. 28).

ROLLING TABLES

For woodworkers who are looking to expand the crosscutting capacity of their existing saws, rolling tables are available as aftermarket add-ons (see

A CROSSCUT SLED MUST BE MADE OF STABLE MATERIALS. I made mine from high-quality, nine-ply, ½-in.-thick Baltic birch plywood. Although the mid-sized box shown in the illustration on the facing page was made for my Delta Unisaw, the design can easily be adapted to any table size and any size workpiece. The sled's accuracy depends on alignment. Your saw's miter-gauge slots must be parallel to the saw-blade (see p. 100), and the sled's fence must be perpendicular to the blade's line of cut.

Cutting the Parts

Cut out the sled's components to the sizes indicated in the illustration or to fit your own saw. The base should be 1 in. wider than the saw table; the fence and rear rail should match the length of the base.

Laminate the 1-in.-thick fence and rear rail from two pieces of plywood. Joint their bottom edges square, and saw a ⅛-in. by ⅛-in. rabbet along the inside bottom face of the fence for sawdust and chip clearance. On the inner face of the fence and rear rail, cut ¼-in. by ¼-in. dadoes to receive the ends of the blade cover. Next, bandsaw the fence and rear rail to the dimensions given in the illustration, proportioning yours to suit your saw table. The fence is higher in the center for holding workpieces vertically when necessary. The ends of the fence are lower for clamping pieces to the sled.

Make the runners from a hard, stable material such as plastic or metal. Rip the runners to fit snugly side-to-side in the miter-gauge slots, but make them a bit thinner than the depth of the slots so the base sits flat on the table.

Attaching the Base to the Runners

Insert the runners into their slots and place the base on top of them with its front end aligned with the front edge of the saw table and its left edge extending 1 in. beyond the saw table. Mark the base over the centerline of each runner, then drill pilot holes and countersink for #8 x ¾-in. flathead screws about every 4 in.

If the base doesn't glide freely, remove it from the table and take down any high spots on the runners using a scraper or a rabbet plane. When the sled glides well, wax the runners and the underside of the base to reduce friction.

A crosscut sled is a great improvement over a miter gauge in terms of both safety and performance. This sled includes a clear polycarbonate blade cover that can be lifted onto the workpiece before making a cut.

Attaching the Rear Rail and Fence

Fasten the rear rail to the base using #10 x 2-in. flat-head screws spaced about 3 in. apart. Avoid the blade-cover dadoes and the blade path. The rear rail doesn't need to be exactly square to the blade because it's not used as a fence. Next, slide the assembly into its slots and cut a kerf through the base, stopping a few inches short of the front.

For your sled to be accurate, the fence must be absolutely straight, flat, and square to the blade. Use a square to check that the face of the fence is square to the base. If it isn't, joint the bottom edge of the fence and recut the rabbet if necessary.

Squaring the fence to the saw kerf isn't difficult, but it can take some patience. First, mark the position of the fence, setting it about 2½ in. in from the front edge of the base. Next, with the fence removed, turn the base upside down and drill and countersink a screw-clearance hole at the right- and left-hand ends of the fence location. Slightly elongate the left-hand countersink and hole, which will allow you to pivot the fence a bit to adjust its angle later.

Place the sled runners in their grooves so that the front edge of the sled overhangs the table saw. Align the fence to its positioning marks, and lightly clamp it to the base. Using an accurate square, adjust the fence perpendicular to the kerf in the base, then

Crosscut Sled

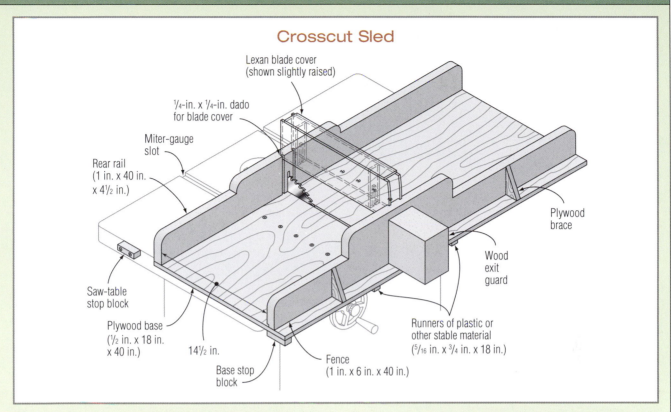

Lexan blade cover
(shown slightly raised)

1/4-in. x 1/4-in. dado
for blade cover

Miter-gauge
slot

Rear rail
(1 in. x 40 in.
x 4 1/2 in.)

Saw-table
stop block

Plywood base
(1/2 in. x 18 in.
x 40 in.)

14 1/2 in.

Base stop
block

Fence
(1 in. x 6 in. x 40 in.)

Plywood
brace

Wood
exit
guard

Runners of plastic or
other stable material
(5/16 in. x 3/4 in. x 18 in.)

tighten the clamps and drive screws through the base into the fence. Now crosscut a wide piece of scrap using the sled.

Afterward, flip one piece over, then butt the ends of the two pieces together with their edges against the fence to check the cut for square as when testing the squareness of the blade to the table (see the top illustration on p. 95). If the fence needs adjustment, loosen the screw in the elongated hole, adjust the fence angle, and recut and check the test piece again. When the cut is square, fix the fence in place with screws spaced about 3 in. apart.

Triangular plywood braces help keep the fence rigid and square to the base. Glue and clamp them about 8 in. in from the ends of the sled to allow clamping space for attaching an extension fence for repetitive crosscutting.

Making the Blade Cover and Stop Blocks

The blade cover for the crosscut sled is a necessity. It protects your fingers and shields you from offcuts and sawdust thrown by the blade. I made my cover from 1/4-in.-thick Lexan, an impact-resistant polycarbonate,

but you could also use a clear acrylic plastic like Plexiglas®. Cut the parts to size on the table saw and assemble them using a suitable adhesive. Check your local phone directory for plastics suppliers, who can supply you with material and the necessary solvent.

After assembly, sand a slight crown on the ends of the cover to allow it to move up and down easily in the sled's fence and rear rail dadoes (see the photo on p. 170).

Because the blade passes through the fence for all crosscuts, make a solid-wood exit guard to protect your fingers. The guard should be at least 2 in. thick and at least 1/4 in. taller than the blade at maximum height. It should also extend at least 1 in. past the fully raised blade when top dead center of the blade intersects the face of the fence. Glue and clamp the guard to the sled with the long-grain surface against the fence.

Fasten the stop blocks to the base and the saw table as shown to prevent sawing through the exit guard. The saw-table stop block should stop the sled when top dead center of the blade meets the face of the fence.

An aftermarket sliding, or rolling, table attaches to the side of a saw, providing increased crosscutting capacity. Although these rolling tables make handling large stock much easier, they are not as accurate as an integral sliding table that comes right up to the sawblade.

the photo above). Often referred to as sliding tables, these attachments might be more properly called rolling tables because their mechanisms are significantly different from those used on integral sliding tables.

As opposed to an integral sliding table, a rolling table typically attaches to the left side of a saw table, leaving some distance between the blade and the table, somewhat affecting accuracy and workpiece drag. Although a rolling table is not as accurate or solid as an integral sliding table, it is a big improvement over a miter gauge, especially for long or wide workpieces.

Like the fence on an integral sliding table, the fence on a rolling table can easily be adjusted to any angle for sawing miters or compound bevels on the ends of workpieces. All rolling-table fences include drop-stops for convenient repetitive cutting.

Basic Crosscutting Techniques

Although I do most of my crosscutting on a sliding table these days, I'll describe techniques for using a miter gauge as well as a crosscut sled. A crosscut sled is an immense improvement over a miter gauge, and I strongly recommend that you make or purchase one.

SETTING UP FOR THE CUT

Mount the appropriate blade on your saw. For most crosscutting, except sawing plywood, use a high-quality 40- to 60-tooth ATB blade. (For more on blades, see chapter 3.) Set the blade height as described on p. 127. Move your rip fence to the outer end of the table or remove it from the table entirely so it won't interfere with the cut or cause offcuts to gather near the blade. Never use the rip fence itself as a stop block—the offcut may wedge between the blade and the fence, causing kickback. Remember to wear safety glasses and ear protection.

When cutting with a miter gauge, hold the workpiece against its fence, aligning the cutline on the workpiece with the edges of the teeth on the appropriate side of the blade. If you're using a miter gauge with an auxiliary fence that extends right up to the blade, you can align the cutline with the end of the fence. Or you could mark the table in line with the blade, then align your cutline to that. However, after a little practice, you should have no trouble simply sighting across the cutline to the blade.

When using a crosscut sled, a stock blade guard would get in the way, so I outfitted my crosscut sled with a custom guard (see the sidebar on pp. 148–149). I lift the guard up, align my cutline with the kerf in my sled base, then rest the guard on the workpiece.

MAKING THE CUT

When you're ready to cut, stand to the same side of the blade as the miter gauge. If you're using a crosscut sled, stand to the side of the blade opposite the offcut. This position is safer and makes for easier pushing. Turn on the saw and allow the blade to reach full speed.

If you are using a miter gauge, use one hand to hold the workpiece against the fence while the other hand pushes the gauge forward into the blade. Don't be tempted to hold the offcut half of the workpiece—a dangerous move. When using a crosscut sled, hold the workpiece against the fence with one hand while making sure to keep your other hand out of the path of the blade.

Feed the workpiece into the blade at a steady, continuous speed. Crosscutting offers less resistance than ripping, so the tendency is to feed the work quickly. However, the proper feed speed depends on the thickness and density of the material being cut. When crosscutting, you should generally feed a workpiece a bit slower than you would when ripping the same piece of wood. When the cut is complete, return the workpiece and fence to their starting point. Slide the wood slightly away from the blade on the return stroke to avoid touching the blade.

Even if your miter gauge is set square to the blade, it's wise to check the sawn end with a square. Sometimes inconsistent feed pressure can cause the workpiece to veer just a bit from a straight line.

Make Sure End Is Square

When crosscutting stock to length, first square one end of the workpiece. The temptation here is to trim off only 1/16 in. or so, or just enough to square up the end. The problem is that if the blade is cutting only on one side, it can deflect, cutting the end out of square. It's best to cut in far enough from the end to leave a fully sawn offcut.

Repetitive Crosscutting

Making repetitive cuts to the same length is a common practice in woodworking. There are several ways to approach this on a table saw. Most setups involve employing a stop block set at the desired distance from the blade, eliminating the need for marking cutlines on individual pieces and ensuring pieces of exactly the same length.

Remember that the first step in cutting a workpiece to finished length is to saw one end square. This will be the end that abuts the stop block for the finished cut. One approach to cutting repetitive pieces is to first cut one end square on every piece. Next, fix a stop block to your miter-gauge auxiliary fence or sled fence and saw the pieces to final length while butted against the stop. The problem with this approach is that it involves handling every piece twice. There are better methods.

USING POSITIONING STOP BLOCKS

One method is to use a long, L-shaped stop block that sits well forward of the blade and simply positions the workpiece on the miter-gauge fence for the final cut. The first step is to cut one end of a workpiece square, disregarding the stop block, which is clamped in place but out of the way. Next, turn the workpiece end-for-end, butt the squared end against the stop block, then push the workpiece forward into the blade (see the photo below).

One way to make repetitive cuts for longer pieces is to position the workpiece on the miter-gauge fence using a long L-shaped stop block. First, crosscut one end of a workpiece square without using the stop, then butt the squared end against the stop before pushing the workpiece into the blade for the second cut.

Repetitive cuts can be made by clamping a thick positioning block to the rip fence well in front of the blade.

A drop-stop allows easy, accurate repetitive crosscutting. First, one end of a workpiece is squared with the stop flipped up out of the way. Then the stop is dropped down in place for cutting pieces to final length, as shown here.

An alternative approach is to clamp a positioning stop to the rip fence well in front of the blade (see the top photo). Make sure the stop is thick enough to allow plenty of room between the end of the workpiece and the fence to prevent trapping the cut piece in a small space between the fence and the blade.

The disadvantage to using positioning blocks is that the workpiece can slip as you feed it forward. Unless you hold it very firmly during its travel, you can end up with miscuts. When cutting multiples, I've never hit 100 percent accuracy with this method. A better approach is to use drop-stops.

USING DROP-STOPS

A drop-stop provides the advantage of being able to flip a stop up out of the way when necessary without moving the stop's position on the fence. This way, you can flip the stop up to make the initial squaring cut on a piece of stock, then drop it down to make the final cut. When down, the stop holds the workpiece in position against the fence, making for very accurate cuts (see the bottom photo on p. 153).

Drop-stops are available commercially for attachment to an auxiliary miter-gauge fence or crosscut sled (see Sources on p. 197). Many after-market miter gauges come equipped with drop-stops, as do the fences on most sliding and rolling tables.

USING A CROSSCUT SLED

When using a crosscut sled for repetitive cuts, you don't necessarily need a drop-stop. Instead, you can clamp a fixed stop block to the fence at the proper distance from the blade, then make your initial squaring cut with the workpiece riding on the opposite end of the sled (see the photo below left). Afterward, slide the workpiece against the stop to make the final cut (see the photo below right). The stop block should be notched at the bottom to provide clearance for chips and dust.

For repetitive crosscutting using a crosscut sled, first square one end of the workpiece from the right side of the sled.

Next, slide the workpiece over against the stop block to crosscut it squarely to final length.

For repetitive cutting of pieces that are longer than the sled fence, clamp an extension board to the fence, then clamp a stop block to the extension board.

To cut pieces that are longer than the sled fence, you can mount a stop block to an extension fence that's clamped to the sled fence (see the photo above). Make your fence extension from a light, stable wood such as poplar or mahogany. The extension should be thick enough to prevent flex and tall enough to clamp to the fence above the workpiece.

Crosscutting Wide Panels

Accurate crosscutting of wide panels requires some form of solid support to carry the workpiece through the blade. A miter gauge is out of the question in a lot of cases because the operation is too awkward. A sliding table is the best option, but if you don't have one, a crosscut sled will really shine here too.

The procedure is basically the same as for standard crosscutting but with a larger sled. With the guard in place, square off one end of the panel, mark it for length, then align your cutline to the kerf in your sled to make the final cut. On very wide work, I sometimes start the cut by raising the spinning blade up into the workpiece. This can be safer than suspending a large sled in front of the saw in order to begin the cut in front of a raised blade.

If your workpiece is both wide and long (such as a large tabletop or case side), you may need an auxiliary stand or table to the side of the saw

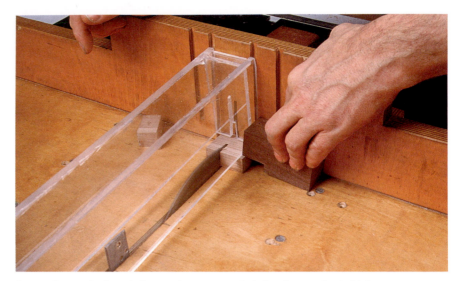
Crosscut very short workpieces using a crosscut sled and a wooden hold-down.

You can crosscut wide panels using a large sled. A wood block clamped to the fence holds long boards down against the base of the sled.

to support the overhanging panel. When the overhang isn't too great, my preferred method is to clamp a thick block of wood to the sled fence to keep the workpiece from lifting (see the top photo).

You'll also need some form of outfeed support to carry the sled as it leaves the rear of the table. Although you can use an auxiliary stand or boards clamped to sawhorses, the best solution is an outfeed table. Mine has grooves that line up with the miter-gauge slots in the saw table (see the photo on p. 120).

Crosscutting Short Pieces

Crosscutting short pieces on the table saw can be dangerous because it can place your fingers too close to the blade. The safest way to crosscut short pieces is with a crosscut sled. Use a wooden hold-down to secure the work-piece down and against the fence, and make the cut with the blade cover in place (see the botom photo on the facing page).

You could also cut short pieces using a hold-down against your miter-gauge auxiliary fence, but the guard can't be used for this operation, and a small piece is more difficult to handle like this. One other option, of course, is to cut short pieces to length using a handsaw at your workbench.

Crosscutting Bevels

Bevel crosscuts, sometimes called end miters, are produced by crosscutting a board with the sawblade tilted at an angle other than 90 degrees. This is a joinery cut that I typically use only for joining molding, although it can also be used for deep picture frames and cases with mitered corners. Because the face of the bevel is basically end grain, the joint needs rein-forcement with a spline or biscuits for strength.

To make a bevel crosscut, tilt the blade to the desired angle (usually 45 degrees) and check the setting with a bevel gauge or drafting triangle. For the cleanest cut, set up the workpiece so that the offcut ends up below the blade (see the illustration below).

You can use a miter gauge to crosscut bevels, but for the sake of accu-racy, I use a small crosscut sled with a wide blade slot for cutting dadoes and bevels (see the photo on p. 170). (I don't use this sled for cutting 90-degree angles because offcuts can drop into the opening unless it's cov-ered with a sheet of thin plywood.)

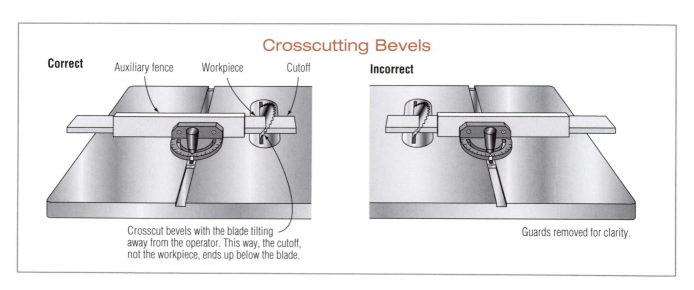

Crosscutting Bevels

Correct Auxiliary fence Workpiece Cutoff

Incorrect

Crosscut bevels with the blade tilting away from the operator. This way, the cutoff, not the workpiece, ends up below the blade.

Guards removed for clarity.

Crosscutting Miters

Miters are produced by feeding the workpiece into the blade at an angle other than 90 degrees. When the sawblade is set at 90 degrees to the table, the cut is called a face miter or flat miter. When the sawblade is set at an angle other than 90 degrees, the cut becomes a compound miter. Miter cuts are made primarily for joinery work (see p. 188).

(see p. 188)

<table>
<tr><td>Test Miter Setup</td></tr>
</table>

When setting the blade or miter gauge to make angled cuts, always make a test cut first and check it using a miter square or bevel gauge.

When cutting miters with a miter gauge, use an auxiliary fence and a stop block.

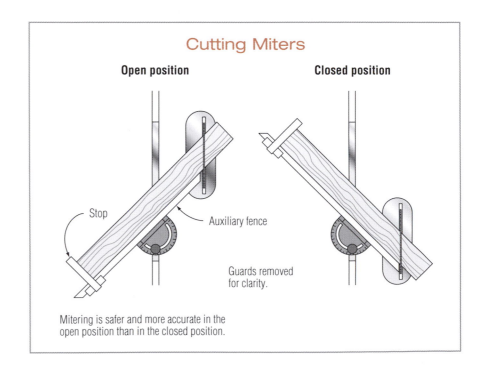

Cutting Miters

Open position

Closed position

Stop

Auxiliary fence

Guards removed for clarity.

Mitering is safer and more accurate in the open position than in the closed position.

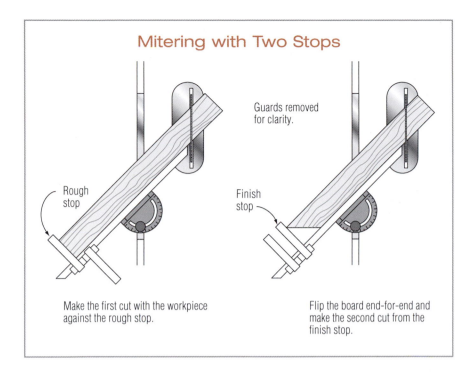

Mitering with Two Stops

Guards removed for clarity.

Rough stop

Finish stop

Make the first cut with the workpiece against the rough stop.

Flip the board end-for-end and make the second cut from the finish stop.

USING A MITER GAUGE

There are a number of ways to set the angle of the miter gauge for making miter cuts. One is to use a bevel gauge or drafting triangle to set the required angle between the miter-gauge body and bar. Another way is to scribe the angle on the workpiece, then turn the gauge upside down onto the workpiece and set the angle to the scribe mark. A third method is to use the stops or angle markings on the miter gauge. Whatever method you use, test your setup using a piece of scrap first.

The miter gauge can be set in either the open or closed position (see the illustration on the facing page). I was taught to use the closed position because it allows you to stand more to the side of the blade and the cut is smoother because of the grain orientation. However, the workpiece is more likely to creep in this position and your hands get closer to the blade as the angle increases. I find that using the open position with an auxiliary fence and stop block yields better results (see the photo on the facing page). Glue sandpaper to the fence to help keep the workpiece from slipping.

Most miter cutting involves making frames, with multiple pairs of workpieces cut to the same length. Unless your workpieces have already been cut to finished length, or at least squared on one end, you will need two stops for the following procedure. (Alternatively, you could miter one end of each workpiece first without using a stop, then miter the opposite end using a stop.)

To cut a workpiece, first miter one end square with the piece butted against a rough stop. Next, flip the piece end-for-end and make the second

The best way to cut 45-degree miters is to use a crosscut sled with two fences that are perpendicular to each other and angled at 45 degrees to the blade. A cutout in the sled's rear rail allows you to miter wide workpieces.

cut with the piece against a finish stop (see the illustration on p. 159). Make sure the stop is wider than the workpiece so the tip of the miter will contact it. Since most frames are rectangular, you'll need two setups: one for the long sides and one for the short sides.

USING A CROSSCUT SLED

I find that the miter gauge is inaccurate for cutting miters—joints that leave little room for error. Instead, I use a simple shopmade crosscut sled for that purpose. For those rare occasions when I need to cut an angle other than 45 degrees, I either fiddle with the miter gauge until I get the cuts right or I add a spacer or hold-down to my crosscut sled to hold the workpiece at the correct angle.

My 45-degree crosscut sled works basically the same as my 90-degree crosscut sled except that two fences—set at 45 degrees to the blade and perpendicular to each other—support the workpiece (see the photo above). Opposing miters are cut using the opposing fences. That way, as long as the fences are at 90 degrees to each other, the joint will be at 90 degrees even if both mating miters are slightly off of 45 degrees. For long pieces, you can extend the fences to accommodate stop blocks. For wide stock, simply make a cutout in the rear rail. Of course, you can fit a sled with fences to cut any angle.

A miter sled is a good approach to cutting angles, but if you cut a lot of varying angles in your regular work, I strongly recommend getting a sliding compound miter saw. These saws, which are specifically designed for cutting miters, are available in a wide variety of sizes and prices.

Cutting Joints and Shapes

C risp, accurate joinery is the hallmark of fine woodworking, and the table saw can help you achieve it. The table saw can be used for cutting many joints, more than I could possibly cover here. In this chapter, I have narrowed them down to the ones I am most familiar with and the ones that use the table saw as the main cutting tool.

Shopmade jigs and fixtures make it possible to cut a wide variety of joints on a table saw. Shown here is a simple jig for cutting finger joints.

Making Strong Joints

A STRONG JOINT DEPENDS ON THREE BASIC CRITERIA: a good mechanical fit, proper grain orientation, and glue. For joint strength, mating surfaces must be smooth and free of loose fibers and small air pockets that prevent intimate contact. Long-grain to long-grain contact is necessary because end grain consists mostly of holes surrounded by some wood fiber. These small fibers don't provide much contact, and the holes tend to wick glue away from the surfaces.

In addition to glue, many joints derive strength from their mechanically locking components. Dovetails, finger joints, mortise-and-tenon joints, and others are designed to resist force in at least one direction, even without glue. But for the joints to perform properly, the parts must fit together snugly.

The types of tools you use have a big effect on joint fits and surfaces. Handplanes, chisels, a jointer, and a router generally create smoother gluing surfaces than a handsaw, table saw, or bandsaw. However, a well-tuned table saw equipped with a sharp, appropriate blade can produce a very satisfactory gluing surface. For most of my table-saw joinery, I use a sharp 40-tooth carbide ATB blade (see chapter 3). If I experience tearout when crosscutting, I switch to a finer 60-tooth ATB crosscut blade.

A word of warning before we begin: Old woodworking books and magazines suggest a lot of different procedures besides joinery that are possible on the table saw. But that doesn't necessarily mean that the table saw is the best machine for the job. Avoid operations like gouging out bowls, cutting circles, resawing wide stock, making dowels, and shaping on the table saw. These techniques are inefficient at best and downright dangerous at worst. There are usually safer and better ways to do the same operations.

Butt Joints

Edge-to-edge joints are the simplest of woodworking joints. They are used primarily to make wider panels from narrower boards, as when making tabletops and case sides. Edge joints can be reinforced with splines, dowels, or biscuits, but most modern wood glues are all that is necessary for a strong joint, provided the joint is well made.

EDGE JOINTS

Making a plain edge, or butt, joint is a simple ripping operation that can be followed by smoothing the edge on a jointer. To get a good joint on the saw, use a carbide-tipped blade with minimum side clearance, meaning that the sides of the teeth are nearly parallel to the plane of the blade body. Make sure your rip fence is set parallel to the blade.

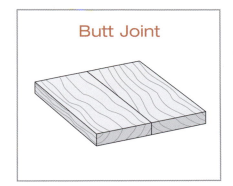

Butt Joint

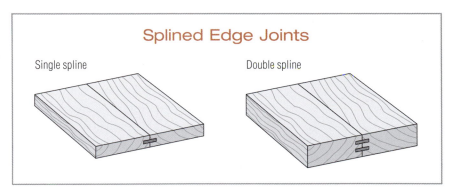

Splined Edge Joints

Single spline

Double spline

Normally, I make my butt joints just a bit concave end-to-end. This is known as a spring joint, and its purpose is to apply more pressure near the ends of the joint, where the end grain absorbs and desorbs moisture more readily than the rest of the panel. The resulting wood movement can cause a joint to fail over time.

You can make a spring joint by ripping a board, then hollowing the edge using a handplane set for a very fine cut. Begin at the center of the board by taking a short pass with the plane. Then take successively longer passes until you've reached the ends of the board. Alternatively, you can spring the joint by using a jointer on which the outfeed table has been adjusted slightly higher than the jointer knives. The maximum gap recommended is a combined $\frac{1}{32}$ in. for 4-ft.-long boards. Shorter boards get less of a gap.

SPLINED EDGE JOINT

Splined edge joints are handy for aligning long boards when making panels or constructing solid-wood cabinet backs. The joints are made by cutting mating grooves in the pieces to be joined, then gluing in a wooden spline when assembling the panel. (The joints are not glued for solid-wood cabinet backs.) The width of the spline is typically equal to half the thickness of the stock being joined but no more than $\frac{3}{4}$ in.

I usually cut the mating grooves with a single sawblade. Material thicker than 1¼ in. calls for two grooves. For grooves wider than $\frac{1}{8}$ in., you can use a dado head. Alternatively, you can cut the grooves after moving the rip fence the width of a saw kerf or by adding a spacer against the rip fence. When making a single, centered groove, you could set the blade off-center, then rotate the stock to make a second cut to widen the groove, but the groove width will vary if the stock isn't all exactly the same thickness.

Begin by marking the face of every workpiece, then mark the center of one workpiece edge, align the edge mark with the center of the blade or dado cutter, and set the rip fence. It's not critical that the groove be exactly centered. Adjust the height of the blade to match half the width of the spline plus about $\frac{1}{16}$ in. for glue space.

Leave Room for Glue

When cutting spline grooves, make sure they are deep enough to allow about $\frac{1}{16}$ in. of extra space for glue after the spline is inserted.

To cut the grooves, feed the workpiece on edge over the blade, using a tall auxiliary fence to support wide stock. Set a featherboard against the stock right at the blade where it will do double-duty as both a hold-down and a guard. For long stock, a long board clamped across the saw table will do a better job than a featherboard (see the photo below). To ensure that the grooves line up exactly with each other, always feed the marked face of every workpiece against the fence when cutting.

Make your splines from plywood or solid wood. Because of its cross-grain construction, plywood makes stronger splines than those ripped from solid wood. I use solid wood when making spline-and-groove cabinet backs because the splines are visible when the boards shrink.

When grooving the edge of a long workpiece for splining, a long board clamped across the saw table will keep the workpiece pressed to the fence for an accurate cut.

Safe Joinery

AN INHERENT PROBLEM WHEN CUTTING JOINTS AT A TABLE SAW is the lack of safety equipment for many of the procedures. Many of the joints are difficult or impossible to cut using stock guards because you often have to handle workpieces on end, on edge, and at odd angles. However, it's not too difficult to devise guards for most joinery procedures, as you'll see from the examples in this chapter. An ingenious woodworker will be able to come up with additional solutions as well.

A spline should fit snugly in its groove, requiring only hand pressure to insert it; if it's too fat, the joint will spread. The spline should be slightly less wide than the combined width of the grooves. If it's too wide, the joint won't pull together; if it is too narrow, strength is compromised. Easing the spline's edges a little using a sanding block eliminates any splinters that might interfere during glue-up.

HIDDEN SPLINE JOINT

A hidden spline joint is the same as a splined edge joint, except that the groove stops short of the ends of the board. It's a useful joint when you want to conceal the spline and groove at the end of a tabletop, for example.

You make the cut in the same way as sawing a through groove except that stop blocks clamped to the rip fence register the workpiece for the desired length of the groove. The workpiece is butted against the forward stop, lowered onto the spinning blade, then pushed until the workpiece butts against the rear stop (see the top illustration on p. 166). This kind of "drop-in" cutting is safe as long as the groove is shallow and narrow. Don't try it with a dado or molding head set for a deep cut. Make sure to use a tall auxiliary fence to support wide workpieces on edge.

To set up for the cut, begin by laying out the beginning and end of the groove on one of your workpieces. Extend the layout lines onto one face of the workpiece. You'll use these lines to set up your stop blocks. Next, raise the blade or dado head to the desired height, then move the fence against it. Using a pencil and square, mark on the fence the points at which the teeth at the front and rear of the blade pass through the throat plate. These marks indicate the beginning and end of the cutting arc.

Move the rip fence the desired distance from the cutter, and lower the blade. Place the workpiece on the table so that the mark on the leading end is aligned with the mark on the rip fence at the rear of the blade. Then clamp a stop block to the fence against the trailing end of the workpiece. Next, position the workpiece so that the mark on its trailing end aligns with the fence mark at the front of the blade. Clamp a stop block to the fence against the leading end, raise the blade, and you're ready to cut.

Turn on the saw and guide the workpiece straight down against the fence and the forward stop. Using a featherboard as described on p. 77 will help guide the workpiece onto the blade. Continue with the cut until the workpiece abuts the rear stop, then carefully lift the workpiece up from the trailing end first.

If your workpiece is longer than the capacity of the rip fence, you won't be able to use stop blocks. Instead, you can work to marks made on the saw table. Large workpieces will be heavy enough to counteract the throwing force of the blade as you lower the workpiece onto it.

Once the groove is cut, you can square off its ends to accept a square-ended spline, or you can shape the ends of the spline to match the contours at the ends of the grooves.

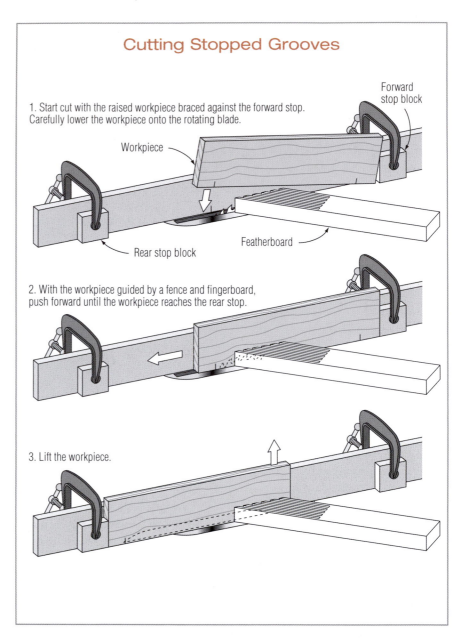

Cutting Stopped Grooves

1. Start cut with the raised workpiece braced against the forward stop. Carefully lower the workpiece onto the rotating blade.

Forward stop block

Workpiece

Rear stop block

Featherboard

2. With the workpiece guided by a fence and fingerboard, push forward until the workpiece reaches the rear stop.

3. Lift the workpiece.

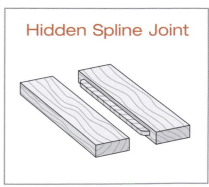

Hidden Spline Joint

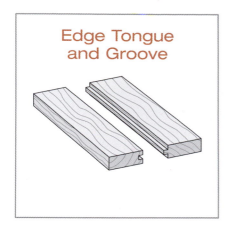

Edge Tongue
and Groove

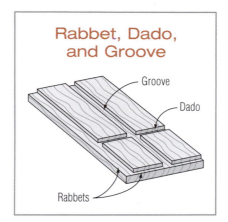

Rabbet, Dado,
and Groove

Groove

Dado

Rabbets

EDGE TONGUE-AND-GROOVE JOINT

Cutting a rabbet on both sides of the edge of a board will create a tongue that can fit into a groove in the mating board. Edge tongue-and-groove joints are often used to construct solid-wood cabinet backs that are made up of multiple boards. The edges are left unglued to allow the back to expand and contract.

To make the joint, cut the groove first, centering it on the edge of the board. In width, it should equal one-third of the board's thickness. Make it about half as deep as the board is thick. Cut the groove as you would a splined edge joint (see p. 163).

To make the mating tongue, cut two opposing rabbets on the edge of the mating board. You can cut the rabbets using a single blade or a dado head as described on pp. 168-170. If the boards are thin enough to make the opposing rabbets in one operation, you can cut the tongue using two blades held apart with a spacer of wood, plastic, or metal. This ensures tongues of consistent thickness, regardless of inconsistencies in the stock thickness.

Rabbets, Dadoes, and Grooves

Three types of cuts—the rabbet, the dado, and the groove—are frequently used in construction of furniture and cabinets, and all of them can be cut on a table saw. A rabbet is a square-sided cut made on the edge or end of a board. A dado is a square-sided slot that runs across the grain in the face of a board. A groove is shaped like a dado but runs parallel to the grain on either the face or edge of a board. Nowadays, woodworkers often make these cuts using a router, but there are advantages to cutting them on a table saw: You can make deeper cuts in a single pass, and the table saw can be better than the router for cutting to exact width if routing would require multiple passes.

Use Offcuts for Tests

Many setups for joinery require test cuts—you want to be sure the setup is accurate before you ruin good wood. The best source for test pieces is offcuts from the stock you milled for your project. If you need long test pieces, be sure to mill extra stock when you're milling your workpieces.

RABBET

A rabbet is often cut into the rear edges of case sides to accept a frame-and-panel, plywood, or tongue-and-groove cabinet back. Cabinet doors can be rabbeted on the back side for half-overlay mounting, and if the cabinet frame is rabbeted as well, the edges of the door and frame will fit together to form a dustproof door joint. You can also cut a rabbet or rabbets to create a tongue that fits into a dado or groove.

There are two basic approaches to cutting a rabbet on a table saw: in two passes using a single sawblade or in one pass using a dado blade.

Two-pass method To cut a rabbet in two passes using a single blade, feed the workpiece on edge to cut the first rabbet shoulder, then cut the

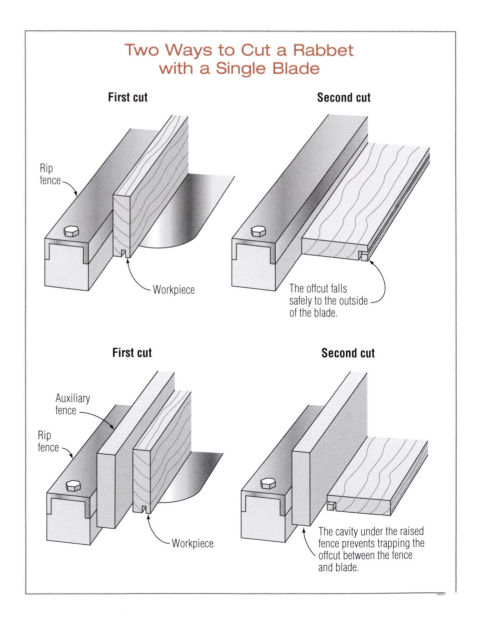

Two Ways to Cut a Rabbet with a Single Blade

First cut

Rip fence

Workpiece

Second cut

The offcut falls safely to the outside of the blade.

First cut

Auxiliary fence

Rip fence

Workpiece

Second cut

The cavity under the raised fence prevents trapping the offcut between the fence and blade.

second rabbet shoulder by feeding the piece flat on the saw table, as shown in the illustration on the facing page. One approach is to set the saw up so that the offcut is freely released on the side of the workpiece opposite the blade. This method is fine for workpieces that are all the same width. If they're not, you must readjust the fence every time you cut a board of a different width.

A better approach for rabbeting workpieces of different widths is to position the stock so the rabbeted edge is against the fence. The advantage here is that you don't have to readjust the fence setting to cut the second shoulder on pieces of different widths. To prevent trapping the offcut between the blade and the fence, use an auxiliary fence that is raised above the saw table enough to allow the cutoff to fall freely away from the blade.

To cut a rabbet on the end of a board, either use a dado head, feeding the workpiece on the flat with a crosscut sled or a miter gauge equipped with an auxiliary fence. Alternatively, you could rout the rabbet.

Dado-head method If you have a lot of pieces to rabbet, it's a lot easier to cut the joint in a single pass using a dado head. You make the cut with the workpiece held flat on the table by a wooden hold-down/ guard (see the photo below). You'll also need a wooden auxiliary fence attached to the rip fence and a throat plate to accommodate your dado blade.

The safest, most accurate way to cut rabbets using a dado head is to clamp a board to the rip fence above the workpiece where it can serve as a hold-down and blade guard.

When cutting dadoes, feed the workpiece across the blade using a miter gauge or cross-cut sled.

To make the cut, set up the dado head so it's a little wider than the rabbet to be cut. Lower the blade below the saw table, and adjust your rip fence so the distance between the fence and the far side of the blade equals the width of the rabbet. Next, raise the blade to a height equal to the depth of the rabbet. This will bury the inner section of the dado head in the auxiliary fence. Feed the workpiece over the blade to cut the rabbet. To cut a rabbet wider than the capacity of the dado head, move the fence over for a second cut.

To cut an end rabbet with a dado head, guide the workpiece with a miter gauge or crosscut sled. If you experience crosscut tearout, make a light scoring cut first, with the blade raised just a hair above the table.

HOUSED DADO

A housed dado is frequently used to attach a shelf or drawer-support frame to a case side. The housed dado is not a particularly strong joint mechanically, but as long as the case is held firmly together, it can support a lot of weight.

To cut a housed dado joint in plywood, set the width of a dado blade equal to the thickness of the stock that is to fit into the dado. When

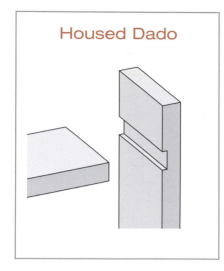

Housed Dado

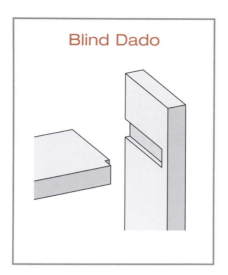

Blind Dado

working with solid wood, plane the stock to fit the dado. Set the blade height equal to the required depth of cut, which should be about one-third the thickness of the piece. You can use a miter gauge fitted with an auxiliary fence to cut the dado, but I prefer to use a crosscut sled with a wide saw kerf designed specifically for dado cutting (see the photo on the facing page).

BLIND DADO

The blind dado is used where an exposed dado joint would be unattractive or where an inset cabinet door requires inset shelves. In a blind-dado joint, the dado is cut only partway across the board. The arc at the end of the cut is typically squared off with a chisel, and a corner is notched out of the mating board to cover the front end of the dado.

Because blind dadoes are normally stopped on one end only, you can feed the workpiece flat into the blade from the opposite end. If a dado is stopped on both ends, it's best to rout it rather than saw it. Dropping work onto a spinning dado head is a dangerous operation and should be avoided.

To set up for the cut, first determine the desired length of the dado. Raise the dado head to the correct height, and mark the point where the front of the dado head protrudes from the saw table. Measure forward from this point a distance equal to the length of the desired dado, then place a stop in line with the blade at this point, as shown in the top illustration on p. 172. (If you use a crosscut sled, you'll need to stop the sled, not the workpiece.) Advance the workpiece into the blade when the front edge contacts the stop.

Apply Downward Pressure

Because a dado head is removing a lot more wood than a single blade, it tries to push the workpiece upward and toward the operator. For safety, feed the stock slowly over the cutters, applying downward pressure so that the work does not climb or lift off the blade. Never place your hands on the workpiece directly over the blade.

Cutting a Blind Dado

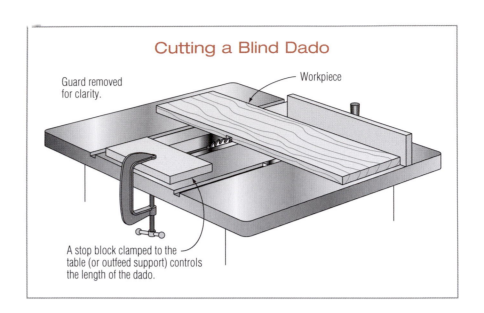

Guard removed
for clarity.

Workpiece

A stop block clamped to the
table (or outfeed support) controls
the length of the dado.

Corner Dado

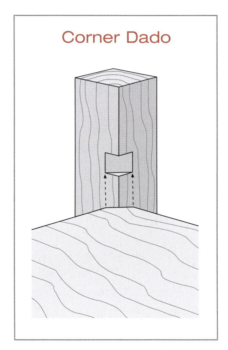

Full Tongue and Dado

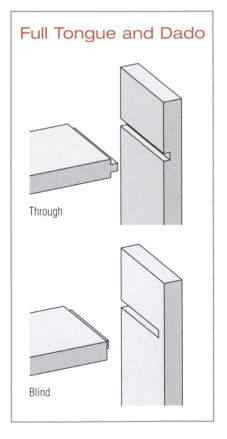

Through

Blind

CORNER DADO

A corner dado is used to house a shelf in the legs of a table or cabinet. A shallow dado cut across the inner corner of the leg accepts the corner of the shelf, which is trimmed off at 45 degrees to fit in the dado. This joint isn't very strong by itself, so you should reinforce it with a dowel.

To cut a corner dado, make a simple V-block jig for holding the workpiece (see the photo below). My jig includes a clear blade guard on the leading edge. Set the blade to the desired height, and guide the jig and workpiece over the blade using a miter gauge.

TONGUE AND DADO

A tongue-and-dado joint is similar to a housed or blind-dado joint except that a tongue is cut on the end of the board that meets the dado. This joint is used primarily to join shelves to case sides. The tongue's shoulders hide the joint and allow the workpieces to be sanded before glue-up without affecting the fit of the joint. The shoulders also add strength.

The joint is usually made with a blind dado, as described on p. 171. Cut the tongue by making two opposing end rabbets, as explained on p. 168.

Bare-faced tongue and dado   A tongue that is offset to one side is referred to as a bare-faced tongue. A bare-faced tongue-and-dado joint is

A V-block jig holds the workpiece for cutting a corner dado.

often used to join drawer and case corners. Although not an exceptionally strong joint, it's fine for many purposes and easy to make. The offset tongue increases the joint's strength by maximizing the stock between the dado and the end of its workpiece.

As a rule, the depth of the dado and the thickness of the tongue are equal to one-quarter the thickness of their respective parts. For example,

Cutting a Bare-Faced Tongue and Dado

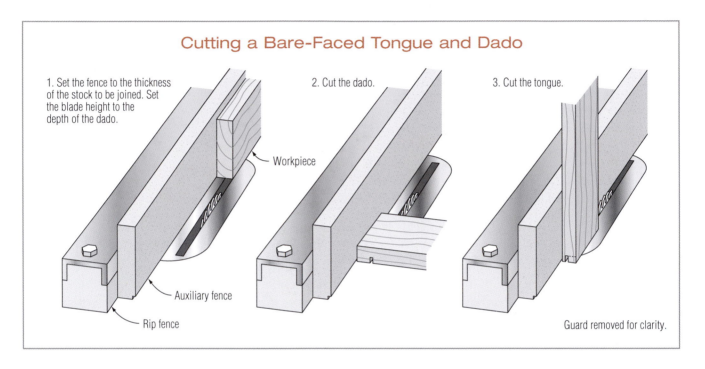

1. Set the fence to the thickness of the stock to be joined. Set the blade height to the depth of the dado.

Workpiece

Auxiliary fence

Rip fence

2. Cut the dado.

3. Cut the tongue.

Guard removed for clarity.

Bare-Faced Tongue and Dado

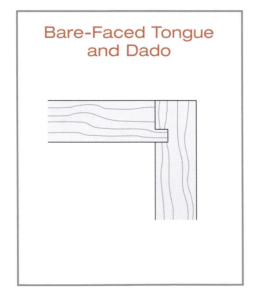

Bare-Faced Tongue and Groove

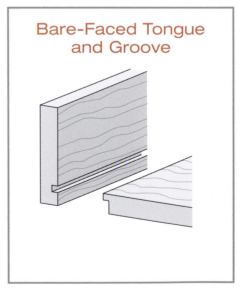

a ¾-in.-thick piece would have a ¼-in. by ¼-in. tongue with a mating dado. You can cut the joint with either a dado blade or a single blade. I usually use a single blade, as described below, for cuts that are ¼ in. deep or less.

To cut the joint, first set the fence so that the distance from it to the outside of the blade equals the thickness of the piece with the tongue (see the top illustration on the facing page). Set the blade height equal to the depth of the dado. To cut the dado, guide the workpiece with a miter gauge while holding the end of the workpiece firmly against the fence.

To create the mating tongue, cut the rabbet as described in the previous section. You'll have to reset the fence from your dadoing setup, but you can leave the blade at the same height to produce a tongue that is the same length as the depth of the dado.

BARE-FACED TONGUE AND GROOVE

A tongue-and-groove joint can be similar in construction to a tongue-and-dado joint except that the groove, unlike the dado, runs parallel to the grain. The tongue on this joint can also be bare faced.

You can use a bare-faced tongue-and-groove joint to fit solid-wood drawer bottoms into their grooves. This joint, which is not glued, allows use of a thick drawer bottom without cutting wide grooves in the drawer sides and front. Make the drawer bottoms ⅜ in. to ½ in. thick with a ¼-in.-thick tongue cut along the front and side edges. To make the ¼-in.-wide groove in the sides and front using a standard blade with ⅛-in.-wide teeth, clamp a ⅛-in.-thick spacer stick to the rip fence and cut the first groove. Remove the spacer and make another cut, producing the ¼-in.-wide groove for the drawer bottom.

Dovetail Trade-Off

When you are cutting dovetails on the table saw, the junction of the slot wall and slot bottom won't meet neatly because of the shape of the saw teeth, so you'll have to either overcut or do some cleanup afterward with a chisel.

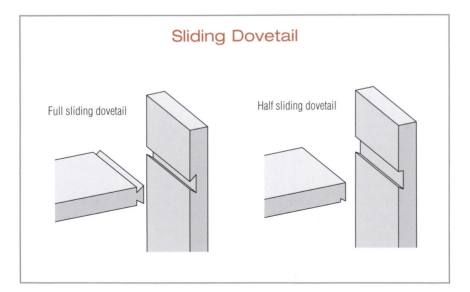

Sliding Dovetail

Full sliding dovetail

Half sliding dovetail

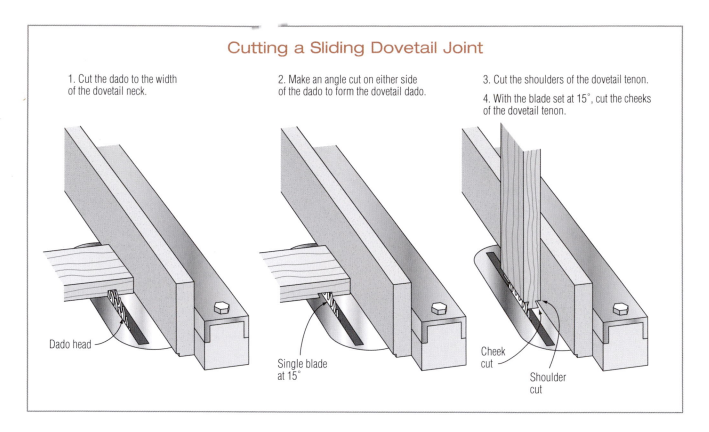

Cutting a Sliding Dovetail Joint

1. Cut the dado to the width of the dovetail neck.

2. Make an angle cut on either side of the dado to form the dovetail dado.

3. Cut the shoulders of the dovetail tenon.

4. With the blade set at 15°, cut the cheeks of the dovetail tenon.

Dado head

Single blade at 15°

Cheek cut

Shoulder cut

Sliding Dovetails

A sliding dovetail joint is similar to a housed dado, but it provides additional mechanical strength in shelf, frame, and drawer construction. Although you can make this joint on a table saw, it's actually much more easily made using a router and router table. The joint can take the form of a full (symmetrical) dovetail or a half-dovetail. The half-dovetail is cut the same way as described below for the full dovetail, except that you make the angle cuts on only one side of the joint.

Make the dovetail slot first, using a dado head as wide as the narrowest part of the tail to remove most of the waste, as shown in the illustration above. Then replace the dado head with a single blade set to an angle of 15 degrees and cut the angled shoulders of the slot.

To cut the tail, first cut the two shoulders using a crosscut sled or miter gauge. Mark a tail test piece directly from the slot, then use the test piece to set up a stop block on the sled fence. The stop block's distance from the blade should equal the depth of the slot. Cut one shoulder, then flip the workpiece over to cut the opposite one. To cut the tail cheeks, set the blade to 15 degrees and feed the workpiece vertically across the blade. Use a tenoning jig to support long workpieces (see the illustration on p. 182).

Make the tail slightly oversized to compensate for inaccuracies in stock thickness, then trim each tail individually either on the saw or using a chisel until you get a good fit.

Lap Joints

Lap joints are simple joints that lend themselves to frame construction. A lap joint consists of two rabbets, two dadoes, or a lap and a dado. Variations include the end lap, the T-lap, the cross lap, the edge lap, and the dovetail lap.

You can cut lap joints exclusively on a table saw using either a single blade or a dado head, but I prefer to team up the table saw and the router for a good, clean cut. Unless you use a very good-quality dado head, the joint surfaces are likely to be rough enough to need further smoothing for a good glue bond.

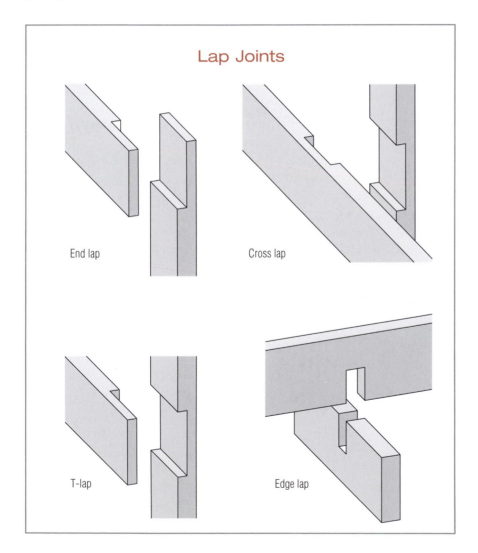

Lap Joints

End lap

Cross lap

T-lap

Edge lap

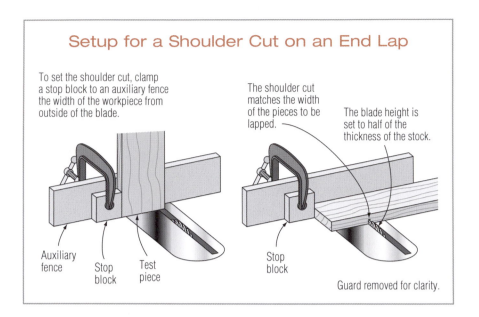

Setup for a Shoulder Cut on an End Lap

To set the shoulder cut, clamp a stop block to an auxiliary fence the width of the workpiece from outside of the blade.

The shoulder cut matches the width of the pieces to be lapped.

The blade height is set to half of the thickness of the stock.

Auxiliary fence

Stop block

Test piece

Stop block

Guard removed for clarity.

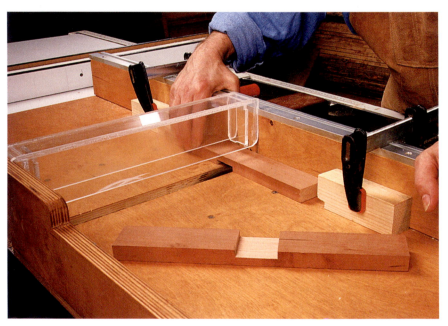

Cut the cross lap using the crosscut sled with stops set to the width of the lap.

Generally, the pieces to be joined are equal in thickness. Therefore, the depth of the cut will equal half the thickness of the workpiece. Use a marking gauge to determine the center of the stock's thickness, then raise the blade to your mark. Make test cuts using scrap the same thickness as the workpieces, then fit them together. Adjust the height of the blade to fine-tune the joint thickness. Remember to leave the joint a bit fat if you'll need to clean up rough joint surfaces. When the depth of cut is set, lay out the actual joint by marking one workpiece on the face and the mating workpiece on the back.

Cut the joints to width using stop blocks. Although you can use an auxiliary fence on the miter gauge, I find it easier and more accurate to use a crosscut sled. Rather than using a ruler to set up stop blocks for an end lap, use a workpiece as a gauge (see the illustration on the facing page). For laps that occur in the middle of a board—such as a cross lap—use two stops to establish the two ends of the lap (see the photo on the facing page).

Bridle Joints

A bridle joint is much stronger than a lap joint because of its mechanical advantage and its increased glue surface. The most common bridle joints are the corner bridle and the T-bridle. The corner bridle is typically used in frame joinery, and the T-bridle is normally used to join an intermediate leg to a table apron.

The corner bridle is basically an open mortise-and-tenon joint. Like any mortise-and-tenon joint, the mortise is cut first, then the tenon is sawn to fit. The open mortise is cut by feeding the workpiece vertically over the blade. To cut the mortise, use a shopmade tenoning jig (see the illustration on p. 182) and a crosscut sled. Clamp the workpiece to the jig, which is clamped to the sled (see the photo on p. 180). I made a simple guard for the sled that allows me to use the tenoning jig without compromising safety. The guard rides in the two dadoes in the rear rail of the sled and is cut out in the front to accommodate the jig and workpiece.

You can cut the tenon shoulders on the table saw, and you can saw the cheeks by either using the tenoning jig or routing. Alternatively, you can saw the cheeks using a dado head as described on p. 168. The opposing dadoes on the cross piece of a T-bridle joint are cut using stops on the crosscut sled, as described previously for making a cross lap joint.

Mortise-and-Tenon Joints

The mortise-and-tenon joint is one of the strongest and most versatile frame joints in the furniture maker's repertoire. It's certainly the joint that I use the most in my work. Variations on the simple tenon include the haunched tenon, through wedged tenon, stub tenon, twin tenon, multiple tenons, and bare-faced tenon. Most of these tenons can be cut on a table saw, although the mortises can't. Mortises are typically routed or drilled and chopped square using a chisel.

Sizing Tenons

As a general rule, the thickness of a tenon should be from one-third to one-half the thickness of the workpiece. When making a blind mortise-and-tenon joint, the tenon should be $\frac{1}{32}$ in. shorter than the depth of the mortise to allow space for excess glue.

Corner Bridle

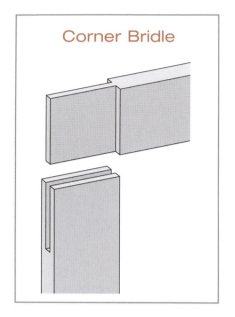

T-Bridle

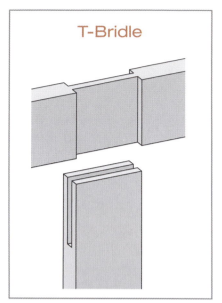

Saw the open mortise for a bridle joint using a tenoning jig clamped to the crosscut sled.

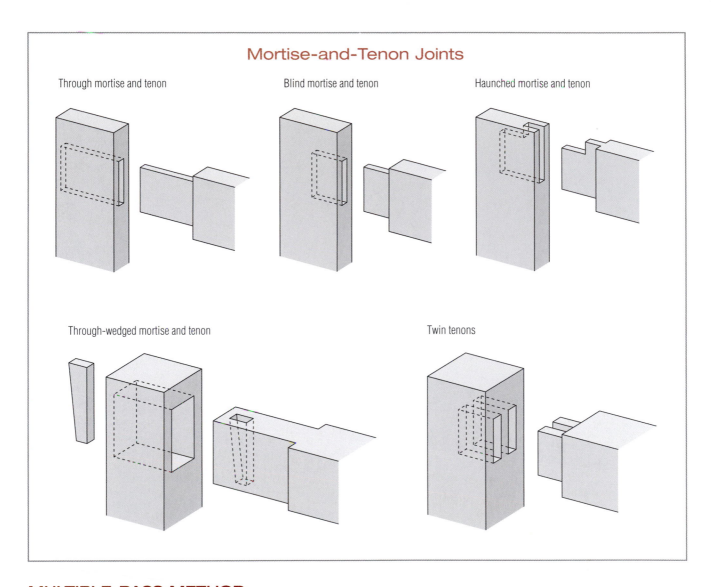

Mortise-and-Tenon Joints

Through mortise and tenon

Blind mortise and tenon

Haunched mortise and tenon

Through-wedged mortise and tenon

Twin tenons

MULTIPLE-PASS METHOD

One of the simplest ways to cut tenons on a table saw is to make a series of passes on either side of the workpiece using a good-quality dado head. The process is the same whether you are using a crosscut sled or a miter gauge. To set up for the multiple-pass method, clamp a stop the required distance from the blade and make a series of passes until the workpiece is butted against the stop. Then flip the piece over and repeat (see the photo on p. 182). For a four-shoulder tenon, finish up by readjusting the height of the blade and standing the workpiece on edge to cut the remaining shoulders.

With this method, any inconsistencies in the thickness of the workpieces will affect the thickness of the tenons. When cutting multiple tenons, it's best to cut them all a bit fat, then trim them to fit with a sharp rabbet plane.

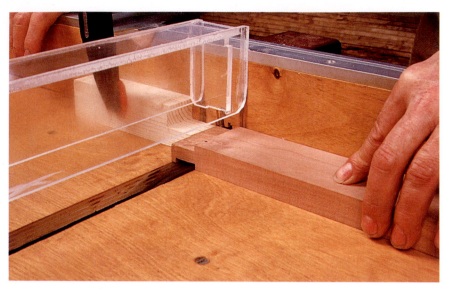

Clamp a stop block to a dado crosscut sled and saw the opposing rabbets to create a tenon. If the tenon is longer than the dado head is wide, make multiple passes.

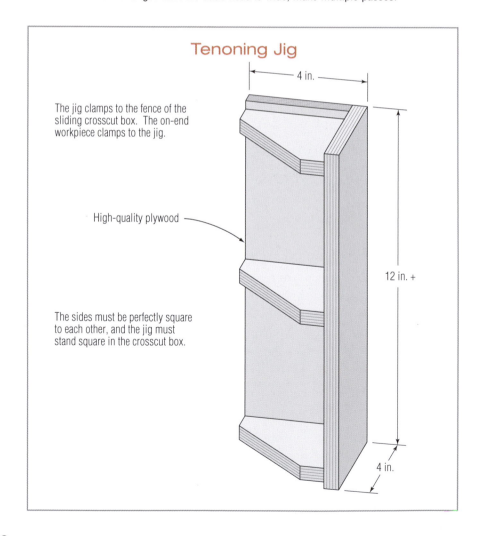

Tenoning Jig

4 in.

The jig clamps to the fence of the sliding crosscut box. The on-end workpiece clamps to the jig.

High-quality plywood

12 in. +

The sides must be perfectly square to each other, and the jig must stand square in the crosscut box.

4 in.

ON-END TENONING

Tenons can be cut with the workpiece standing on end using a tenoning jig (see the illustration on the facing page). You can make the cuts with a single sawblade, flipping the workpiece for the second cut, or with two sawblades and a spacer. Either method is suitable only for pieces that are short enough to handle on end—you clearly wouldn't want to attempt tenoning a bed rail using a tenoning jig. Once the cheeks are cut, cut the shoulders as described on p. 181.

COMBINED METHOD

My preferred method of cutting tenons involves three procedures: cross-cutting the shoulders on the table saw; routing the cheeks on a router table; and rounding the edges of the tenon to fit a routed mortise.

Cut all face shoulders first, using a crosscut sled as described on p. 179. (Leave the stop block in place afterward because you'll use it to cut the edge shoulders later.) Next, rout the cheeks on a router table using the largest-diameter straight bit that your router can safely handle. Set the router table fence so that the bit cuts just shy of the shoulder to avoid side-grain tearout. As always, make test cuts before routing into your workpieces.

Once all of the face cheeks have been routed, return to the crosscut box and use a mortised workpiece as a reference to adjust the blade height for cutting the edge shoulders. Trim all of the edge shoulders by again butting the end of the tenon against your stop block. You can now cut the tenons to final width by hand or on a bandsaw.

Last, round each tenon's corners to approximately match the rounded ends of the routed mortises. After chamfering the corners with a chisel, sand them round using a strip of coarse sanding cloth.

CUTTING PEGS FOR TENONS

To reinforce mortise-and-tenon joints, use square pegs to drive into holes that you've drilled through the joint then chiseled square. To make the pegs, cut them from strips that you've ripped from the edges of long stock. The stock must be square or the pegs will be out of square and therefore undersized. For peg stock, choose straight-grained material that is denser than the wood it is going into.

Install a zero-clearance throat plate on the saw, then set the rip fence to the desired width of the peg stock. For accuracy, use the drill bit that you used to drill the holes as a spacer between the fence and blade, then set the height of the blade slightly less than the diameter of the bit. That way, the strip remains slightly attached to the stock during the cut, preventing it from shooting out of the saw.

Cutting the strips is a two-step operation, as shown in the top illustration on p. 184. Begin by standing the workpiece on edge and cutting all four outside edges, then make the second series of cuts with the face of the

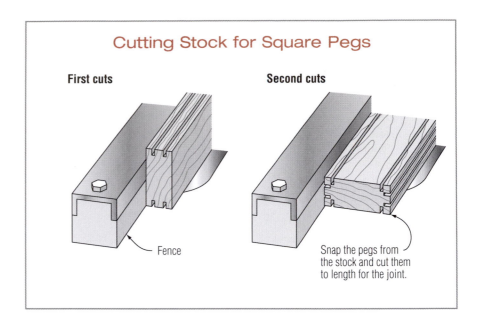

Cutting Stock for Square Pegs

First cuts

Fence

Second cuts

Snap the pegs from the stock and cut them to length for the joint.

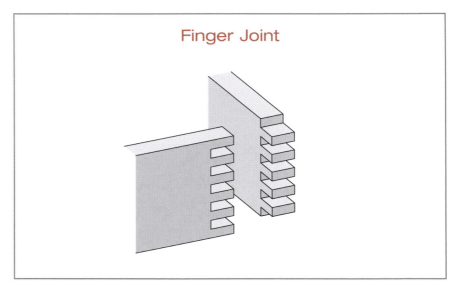

Finger Joint

workpiece flat on the saw table. You can then snap the strips loose from the stock and crosscut to length.

Finger Joints

Finger joints are typically used for boxes, drawers, and other production work. Also called box joints, they are made by cutting a series of equally spaced interlocking slots and fingers into the ends of mating pieces. Finger joints are very strong because of their mechanical connection and large glue surface area.

Finger-Joint Jig

A BASIC FINGER-JOINT JIG CONSISTS OF NOTHING MORE THAN A PLYWOOD BOARD with a protruding key made from hardwood. The key serves as an indexing pin to register every new cut by using the previous cut as a reference.

To make the jig, cut the board to size. Its height isn't critical, but it should be tall enough to support workpieces on end. Next, install on your saw whatever blade you'll use for cutting the finger joints. If you're using a dado head, adjust its width to suit your desired finger width. Adjust the height of the blade to slightly less than the thickness of the stock you'll be cutting, then cut a slot in the board.

Make a hardwood key that fits snugly into the slot and that is long enough to extend well into the workpiece slots you'll be cutting. Glue the key into the slot, and chamfer its top edges slightly.

I made a guard for my jig that stops short of the front fence of my crosscut sled; a piece of wood attached to the rear of the guard is used to clamp the guard to the rear fence (see the top right photo on p. 186).

Finger-Joint Design

Ideally, a finger joint should start and end with the same element, either a slot or a finger. This isn't absolutely necessary, but it restricts any tearout to one face of the workpiece.

A finger joint should begin and end with a full-width finger, so design the width of your project boards to accommodate that spacing. The spacing is especially critical if your fingers and slots are the width of a single sawblade. If you're cutting wider slots using a dado head, you'll be able to adjust the width of the dado head somewhat to suit the width of the stock.

To cut finger joints, I use a jig clamped to the fence of my crosscut sled, but you could clamp it to your miter-gauge jig instead. The jig provides a guide for registering the fingers and slots as you move the stock through the blade (see the sidebar above).

When using the jig, you first need to locate its key precisely one blade width away from the blade. You may have to fiddle some to get this right, but it's critical because even a slight error here will compound across the width of a board, ruining the joint. After measuring off the proper distance, clamp the jig tightly to your miter gauge or crosscut sled and make some test cuts in scrap.

To make the test cuts, set the height of your blade just a hair above the height of the hardwood key. Butt the edge of one test piece against the key and cut the first slot (see the top left photo on p. 186). Slide the first slot over the key to cut the next slot, then cut a few more using the same procedure (see the top right photo on p. 186). Cut a mating scrap piece in the same fashion, then check the fit of the two test pieces together. If the joints are too tight or too loose, adjust the position of the key by shifting the jig slightly to correct the error. You want the pieces to slide together easily with just a bit of hand pressure.

Once you're happy with the joint fit, readjust the blade height to about $\frac{1}{32}$ in. more than the thickness of your workpieces. This will leave the ends of the fingers just a bit proud after the joint is assembled, allowing you to

The first finger-joint slot is made with the workpiece pressed against the projecting hardwood key.

Subsequent slots are cut by registering the previously cut slot over the key.

To establish the location of the first slot in the mating board, place the last-cut slot on the first piece over the key, then place the workpiece edges together.

easily sand them flush. Lock your saw's blade-height handwheel so that all cuts remain the same height. Also, if you are using a miter gauge instead of a crosscut sled, check that the saw's throat plate is level.

Cut your first slot by butting the workpiece against the key, as you did when making your test cuts. Then slot fully across the rest of the board, with each previously cut slot straddling the key to index the workpiece for the next cut. To begin the slots on the mating piece, place the end slot of the previously cut piece over the key and butt its mating piece against it to make the first mating slot (see the bottom photo above).

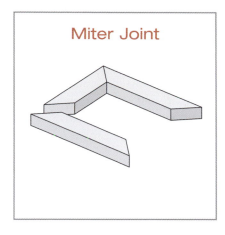

Miter Joint

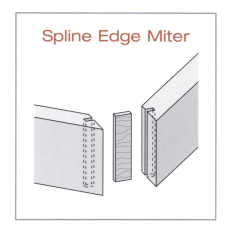

Spline Edge Miter

Jig for a Slip Feather Joint

THIS JIG HOLDS A FRAME ON EDGE AT A 45-DEGREE ANGLE to the sawblade. Make the jig by attaching two 1½-in.-wide fences at 45 degrees to a flat piece of plywood as shown. Trim the two fences at 45 degrees, and attach them with their ends flush to the bottom of the jig. A facing board attached across the fences can serve as a guard, although I usually prefer to use a guard fence clamped to the saw table.

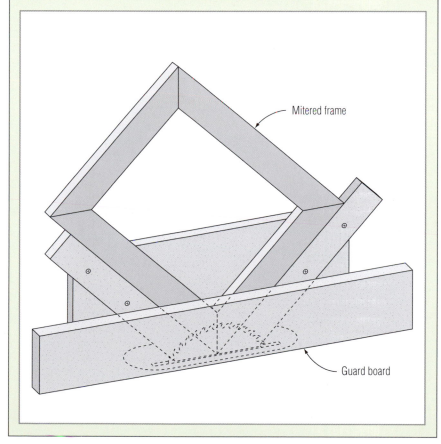

Mitered frame

Guard board

Miter Joints

Miter joints are common in both frame and carcase construction. They're attractive because they show no end grain and if matched well will lead the eye around corners easily. However, being basically end-grain joints, they must be reinforced with splines, biscuits, or some other mechanical attachment. Some miter-joint variations are the spline edge miter, the slip feather, and the mock finger joint. The miters themselves can be cut on a table saw as described on pp. 158–160.

SPLINE EDGE MITER

A spline edge miter incorporates a plywood or solid-wood spline that is glued into mating slots cut into the faces of each miter. For strength, the grain of the spline should run perpendicular to the joint line as shown in the top right illustration on p. 187. For ¾-in.-thick material, a ⅛-in.-thick spline is adequate. Locating the groove close to the inside edge allows you to use a wider spline, which makes for a stronger joint.

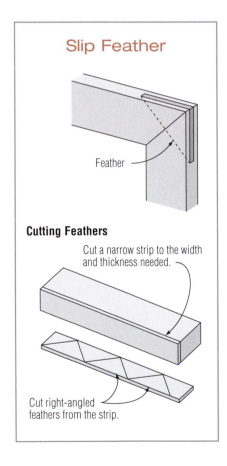

Slip Feather

Feather

Cutting Feathers

Cut a narrow strip to the width and thickness needed.

Cut right-angled feathers from the strip.

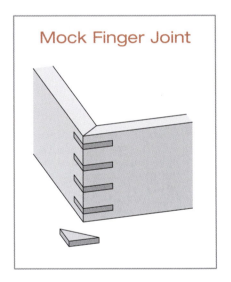

Mock Finger Joint

To cut the slots for a spline edge miter, tilt the blade 90 degrees to the face of the joint. For a typical 45-degree miter, tilt the blade to 45 degrees. Feed the workpiece using a miter gauge while registering the end of the workpiece against the rip fence. Alternatively, you can use a crosscut sled set up with a stop block.

SLIP FEATHER

The slip feather is used to reinforce a mitered frame. The slot for the spline is cut after the frame has been mitered and glued up. Place the glued frame in a jig (see the sidebar on p. 187), and raise the blade so that it will cut just short of the frame's inside corner. For thin material, adjust the fence to make one centered slot. Frames made from stock thicker than 1 in. require two splines per corner.

After cutting the slot, glue in a wooden spline. You can easily make a slip-feather spline by cutting a narrow strip to the required width and

Jig for a Mock Finger Joint

MAKE A V-BLOCK JIG FROM A PIECE OF 2-IN.-THICK STABLE STOCK at least 8 in. wide and about 16 in. long. Rip the V-groove in two passes with the blade tilted at 45 degrees. Leaving at least ¼ in. between the point of the V and the bottom of the block, position the groove so it is closer to one edge than to the other.

Next, cut a slot in the jig to accept the hardwood key. The slot should allow the key to project into the V-groove a bit less than the depth of the slot that will be cut in the box corner. Make a hardwood key that fits snugly into the slot, and glue it in place.

Determine the spacing you want between slots, and make a second slot in the jig. The spacing can be equal to the width of the splines, as in the finger joint, or you can leave larger spaces between the splines. Finally, attach a clear guard to the front of the jig and a solid-wood guard at the rear.

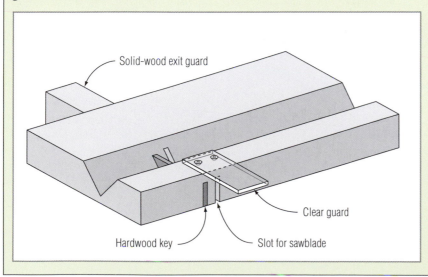

Solid-wood exit guard

Clear guard

Hardwood key

Slot for sawblade

thickness. Each spline is made by cutting opposing 45-degree angles across the stock as shown in the illustration at left on p. 188. You can make the cuts using a miter gauge and auxiliary fence. Use a piece of masking tape on the saw table to gauge the length of the cuts, making the splines a little longer than you need initially. You'll trim them flush to the frame after glue-up.

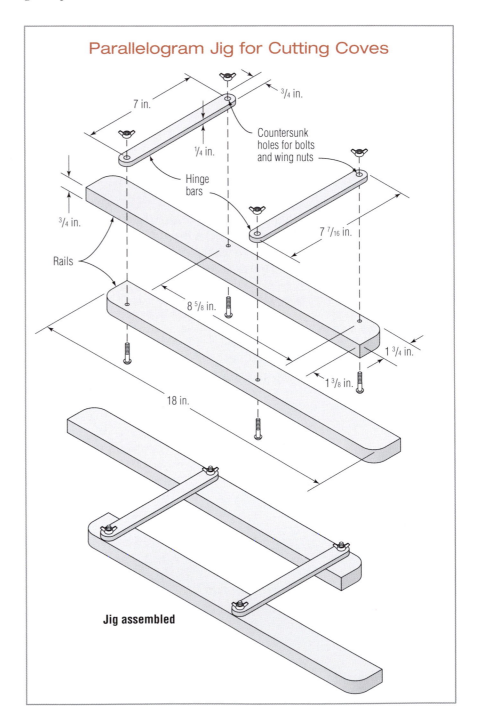

Parallelogram Jig for Cutting Coves

7 in.

3/4 in.

1/4 in.

Countersunk holes for bolts and wing nuts

Hinge bars

3/4 in.

Rails

7 7/16 in.

8 5/8 in.

1 3/4 in.

1 3/8 in.

18 in.

Jig assembled

MOCK FINGER JOINT

The mock finger joint somewhat resembles a standard finger joint but is actually a form of the spline miter. This joint is used on wider boxlike frames and requires using a V-block jig, as shown in the illustration on p. 189.

As with the slip-feather joint, the slots for the mock-finger joint are cut after the box has been glued up. Place the corner of the box in the V-block jig with the edge of the box against the hardwood key, then cut the first slot. Move the box over so the slot fits over the key and make the second cut, just as you did with the finger-joint jig. Continue across the piece until all the slots are cut. Complete the joint by making and gluing in the splines.

Coves

Coves are decorative cuts that I often use to make molding and raised panels. They can be cut on a table saw by clamping an auxiliary fence to the table and feeding the workpiece over the sawblade at an angle. You can cut a wide variety of shapes and sizes by using different sizes of blades and by changing the angle of the fence. Smaller blades produce smaller-diameter coves, and greater fence angles produce steeper curves.

When cutting coves, use a fine-toothed blade. Although you could use a thin-kerf blade, a blade with a thick body will better resist the sideways pressure of the workpiece. If you do a lot of coving, you may want to consider buying a coving head made specifically for this purpose (see the photo on p. 192). To quickly set up your saw for a specific cove, you'll also need to make a parallelogram jig, as shown in the illustration on the facing page.

To set up your saw, begin by laying out the desired cove profile on the leading end of the workpiece. Place the profile next to the blade and raise the blade to equal the finished depth of the cove. Next, use the parallelogram jig to determine the angle for the auxiliary wood fence. To do this, open the jig to the same width as the desired cove, then place it over the blade.

Angle the jig until its two opposing rails just kiss the teeth at the front and rear of the blade. Register the angle on a bevel gauge using an extension stick on the gauge blade (see the top left photo on p. 193). At this angle, clamp an auxiliary fence to the table with the saw teeth pointing toward the fence. Position the fence so that the centerline of the cove will intersect the centerline of the sawblade (see the top right photo on p. 193). To cut a half-cove, position the edge of the fence over the blade centerline (see the bottom photo on p. 193).

To make the cut, lower the blade to about 1/16 in. above the table. You will need to take light cuts because of tooth configuration and side

Sanding Coves

A fter cutting coves on the table saw, you can sand out the saw marks on a lathe, using 100-grit sandpaper wrapped around a shopmade spindle. You could also use a drum sander, a curved scraper, or a custom-shaped sanding block to remove the saw marks.

If you do a lot of coving, a coving head like this one by CMT® produces a smoother cut than a standard sawblade. Its beefy construction also resists the sideways pressure of the workpiece during coving.

stress against the blade. With a guard in place, position the material against the fence and slowly feed the workpiece over the spinning blade. Use a shoe-style pusher (see p. 79), and never put your hands over the top of the blade.

When feeding narrow workpieces, where your hands might be near the blade, jointer-style push pads provide more safety than shoe-style pushers. Make repeated passes, raising the blade about 1⁄16 in. each pass until you've reached the full cove depth.

Kerf Bending

Sometimes wood has to be bent to make curved table aprons, mirror frames, or arched trim for windows or doors, among other projects. To bend wood, you can steam it or stack-laminate it, but there's another alternative: kerf bending. This technique involves cutting a series of equally spaced saw kerfs into the back surface of the stock, which allows the wood to be bent in a curve or circle (see the photo on p. 195). The kerfs stop just short of the stock's thickness, leaving a thin, flexible surface that you can bend as desired.

To establish the fence angle for cutting coves, raise the blade to the cove depth, then place the parallelogram jig over the blade with opposing blade teeth just kissing the edges of the jig as shown. Register the angle using a bevel gauge with an extension stick.

Clamp the fence to the saw table at the registered angle with the saw teeth pointing toward the fence, then make a series of very light passes across the blade.

Cutting a half-cove for a raised panel proceeds much like cutting a full cove except that the sawblade is partially enclosed in the fence.

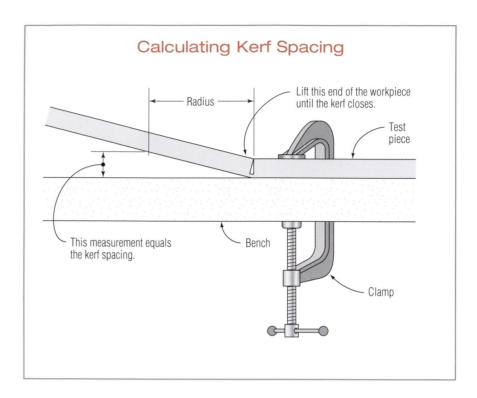

Calculating Kerf Spacing

Lift this end of the workpiece until the kerf closes.

Radius

Test piece

This measurement equals the kerf spacing.

Bench

Clamp

To determine the proper depth and spacing of the kerfs, start out by kerfing a test piece of the same species and dimensions of the finished work. (Some species bend more easily, as does straight-grained, air-dried stock.) Cut the kerfs to within ⅛ in. of the "show" face of the stock, spacing them about ¾ in. apart for starters, then test the flexibility of the piece to get an idea of how much to adjust the kerf spacing. Be aware that widely spaced kerfs can result in flats on the surface of the workpiece. If you want smoother contours, make your kerfs closely spaced.

If you know the radius of the piece you want to bend, you can use a geometric formula that will give you a close approximation of the kerf spacing. First, cut one kerf in a test piece, about ⅛ in. shy of cutting through the stock. Then clamp the kerfed piece on a flat surface, placing the clamp just in front of the kerf. On the opposite side of the kerf, mark a distance equal to the desired radius, then lift the free end of the test piece until the kerf closes (see the illustration above). The distance from the radius mark to the benchtop will approximate the necessary kerf spacing to accomplish the desired radius.

To cut the evenly spaced kerfs, use a crosscut sled with a spacing jig like that used for making finger joints. A nail serves fine for the guide pin. When bending the stock, work slowly to prevent snapping it. Dampening the surface can also help. If the back side of the stock will show, you can cover the kerfs with veneer. To strengthen the workpiece, you can fill the kerfs with epoxy.

Cutting a series of deep, equally spaced kerfs in a workpiece allows it to be bent in a curve or circle for making curved table aprons and other project parts.

Pattern Sawing

Pattern sawing is a useful technique for making exact duplicates of oddly shaped parts that have straight sides. The process involves cutting the workpiece slightly oversize, then attaching to it a pattern that is guided by an auxiliary fence that is aligned with the outer edge of the blade teeth.

Begin by making the pattern from solid wood, plywood, or particleboard. You can bandsaw the multisided shape slightly oversized, then sand or plane the sides straight. Alternatively, you could affix the marked pattern blank to a crosscut sled to make the cuts. When the pattern is complete, trace its shape onto the workpiece, then saw the workpiece slightly oversized.

Secure the pattern to the rough-cut workpiece using small brads that have been clipped off to protrude about ⅛ in. from the pattern. Make sure to nail into what will be the hidden face of the finished workpiece. Alternatively, you can attach the pattern using double-sided tape. Clamp the taped pieces together for a few seconds to ensure a good bond.

Attach an auxiliary fence to your rip fence, positioning it so it will be slightly above the height of the workpiece. The auxiliary fence needs to be wide enough to accommodate any offcuts between the blade and the rip fence. It also needs to be long enough to adequately support the pattern throughout the entire length of the cut. Make sure the fence is parallel to the blade, then align the face of the auxiliary fence with the outside edges of the teeth, as shown in the illustration on p. 196. To prevent cutting

Pattern sawing allows exact duplication of irregularly shaped parts with straight sides. A pattern that's attached to the workpiece rides along an auxiliary fence that is aligned to the sawblade.

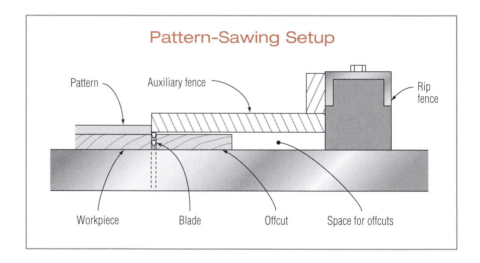

Pattern-Sawing Setup

Pattern

Auxiliary fence

Rip fence

Workpiece

Blade

Offcut

Space for offcuts

through a thin pattern, you can extend the auxiliary fence slightly beyond the blade, but you'll have to reduce the size of your pattern accordingly.

Before making the cuts, adjust the height of the blade to project just a bit above the workpiece thickness, and make sure to use a splitter or riving knife to prevent the offcuts from being violently thrown by the blade (see the sidebar on p. 68). Guide the edges of the pattern along the auxiliary fence, holding the pattern firmly against the fence throughout each entire pass (see the photo above). Stop the saw occasionally to clean away the offcuts.

Sources

Amana Tool® Corp.
120 Carolyn Blvd.
Farmingdale, NY 11735
(800) 445-0077
www.amanatool.com
Sawblades

Biesemeyer Manufacturing Corp.
216 S. Alma School Rd., Ste. 3
Mesa, AZ 85210
(800) 782-1831
www.biesemeyer.com
*Replacement rip fences, blade guards
and splitters, extension tables, sliding
crosscut sleds*

Blue Tornado Cyclones
P.O. Box 156
Buckner, KY 40010
(800) 292-0157
www.bluetornadocyclones.com
Dust collectors

Bridge City Tool Works, Inc.®
5820 N.E. Hassalo
Portland, OR 97213-3644
(800) 253-3332
www.bridgecitytools.com
Layout and measuring tools

Bridgewood®
Wilke Machinery Co.
3230 N. Susquehanna Trail
York, PA
(800) 235-2100
www.wilkemach.com
Table saws

CMT USA
307-F Pomona Dr.
Greensboro, NC 27407
(888) 268-2487
www.cmtusa.com
Table-saw blades

Delta Machinery
(800) 223-7278 (parts or technical
assistance)
www.deltawoodworking.com

DeWalt Industrial Tools
701 E. Joppa Rd., TW 425
Baltimore, MD 21286
(800) 433-9258
www.dewalt.com
Table saws, sawblades

Eagle Tool®
2217 El Sol Ave.
Altadena, CA 91001
(626) 797-8262
www.eagle-tools.com
*Mini-Max European table saws and
combination machines*

Enviro Safety Products
516 E. Modoc Ave.
Visalia, CA 93292
(800) 637-6606
www.envirosafetyproducts.com
Safety supplies

Excalibur Sommerville Group
940 Brock Rd.
Pickering, ON, Canada L1W2A1
(800) 357-4118
www.excalibur-tool.com
Replacement fences, blade covers, rolling tables

Felder® USA
1851 Enterprise Blvd.
West Sacramento, CA 95691
(916) 375-3190
www.felderusa.com
European table saws and combination machines

Fenner Drives®
311 W. Stiegel St.
Manheim, PA 17545
(800) 243-3374
www.fennerindustrial.com
Table-saw link belts

Forrest Manufacturing Company
457 River Rd.
Clifton, NJ 07014
(800) 733-7111
Sawblades

Freud® USA
218 Seld Ave.
High Point, NC 27263
(800) 334-4107
Sawblades

Garrett Wade
161 Avenue of the Americas
New York, NY 10013
(800) 221-2942
www.garrettwade.com
Inca European table saws, table-saw accessories

General® International
835, rue Cherrier
Drummondville, QB, Canada J2b 5A8
(819) 472-1161
www.general.ca
Table saws

Grizzly Industrial®
P.O. Box 2069
Bellingham, WA 98227
(800) 523-4777
www.grizzly.com
Table saws and accessories

Guhdo®-USA, Inc.
1135 JVL Industrial Blvd.
Marietta, GA 30066
(800) 544-8436
www.guhdo.com
Table-saw blades

Hammer® USA
1851 Enterprise Blvd.
West Sacramento, CA 95691
(800) 700-0071
www.hammerusa.com
European table saws and combination machines

HTC® Products, Inc.
120 E. Hudson
P.O. Box 839
Royal Oak, MI 48068
(800) 624-2027
Replacement blade covers, fences, extension tables, tool covers, mobile bases

Incra® Tools
11050 Industrial First
North Royalton, OH 44133
(800) 752-0725
www.woodpeck.com
Replacement fences and accessories

In-Line Industries
661 S. Main St.
Webster, MA 01570
(800) 533-6709
Link belts and accessories

JDS Company
108 Leventis Dr.
Columbia, SC 29209
(800) 480-7269
Air cleaners and accessories

Jet Equipment & Tools®
P.O. Box 1937
Auburn, WA 98071
(800) 274-6848
www.jettools.com
Table saws and accessories

Jointech®, Inc.
11725 Warfield
San Antonio, TX 78216
(800) 619-1288
www.jointech.com
Replacement fences and accessories

Lab Safety Supply
P.O. Box 1368
Janesville, WI 53547
(800) 356-0783
(800) 356-2501 (technical advice)
www.labsafety.com
Safety supplies

Laguna Tools
17101 Murphy Ave.
Irving, CA 92614
(800) 234-1976
www.lagunatools.com
European table saws, combination machines, rolling tables

The L.S. Starrett Company®
121 Crescent St.
Athol, MA 01331
(978) 249-3551
www.starrett.com
Layout and measuring tools

Makita® USA
14930 Northam St.
La Miranda, CA 90638
(310) 926-8775
www.makitaope.com
Table saws

Mesa Vista Design
804 Tulip Rd.
Rio Rancho, NM 87124
(800) 475-0293
www.grip-tite.com
Safety accessories

Modulus 2000 Machinery Inc.
P.O. Box 206
Saint Hubert, QB
Canada J3Y 5T3
(800) 633-8587
www.modulus2000.com
Scoring saw attachments, saw fences, and accessories

Mule Cabinetmaker
519 Mill St.
Lockport, NY 14095
(877) 684-7366
www.mulecab.com
Replacement fences and rolling tables

Oneida® Air Systems
1001 W. Fayette St.
Syracuse, NY 13204
(800) 732-4065
www.oneida-air.com
Dust collectors

Porter-Cable®
4825 Hwy. 45 N.
P.O. Box 2468
Jackson, TN 38302
(800) 487-8665
www.porter-cable.com
Table saws

Powermatic
427 Sanford Rd.
LaVergne, TN 37086
(800) 274-6848
www.powermatic.com
Table saws

Ridgid Tools
Emerson™
P.O. Box 4100
8000 W. Florissant Ave.
St. Louis, MO 63136
(800) 474-3443
www.ridgidwoodworking.com
Table saws and accessories

Rojek
7901 Industry Dr.
North Little Rock, AR 72117
(800) 787-6747
www.tech-mark.com
European table saws and combination machines

Ryobi® Power Tools
5201 Pearman Dairy Rd.
Anderson, SC 29625
(800) 323-4615
www.ryobitools.com
Table saws

Sears Roebuck & Co.
P.O. Box 19009
Provo, UT 84605
(800) 377-7414
www.sears.com
Table saws and accessories

Shopsmith®, Inc.
3931 Image Dr.
Dayton, OH 45414
(800) 543-9396
www.shopsmith.com
Combination machines and accessories

Tenryu® America
4301 Woodland Park Dr., Ste. 104
W. Melbourne, FL 32904
(800) 951-7297
www.tenryu.com
Sawblades

Index

NOTE: page references in *italics* indicate a photograph; references in **bold** indicate an illustration.